Hawaii Cooks...

The
Island Way

Maili Yardley

Topgallant Publishing... Honolulu

Book design and illustrations by Wendy Silva

ISBN 0-914916-62-9

Published By:

TOPGALLANT PUBLISHING CO., LTD.
845 Mission Lane
Honolulu, Hawaii 96813

Manufactured in the United States of America

This Book is fondly dedicated to all you
wonderful people who inspired and shared
so joyously
Mahalo

Table of Contents

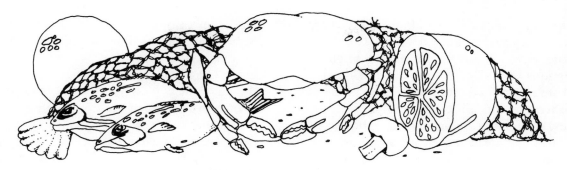

Introduction

INTRODUCTION

The recipes used in this book are a collection from the weekly column, "The Island Way", published in the Honolulu Advertiser and written by the author, Maili Yardley.

Also included are some of the more popular columns in their entirety.

When asked, "What do you mean, 'The Island Way' ", it took but a minute for the author to recall happy, nostalgic impressions that never fade and memories of Hawaii nei that are very much alive.

"The dazzling ocean surrounding us with its *'ehu kai'*, that passing whiff of *limu*, salt, and crabs. . . all God's gifts from the sea.

"Wide, sandy beaches were made for moonlight horseback rides or picnics with bonfires and spontaneous Hawaiian music. . . not just for swimming by day.

"The pungent smell of the open *imu* calling us to a real Hawaiian luau prepared by many loving hands to provide a menu fit for a king that took hours to consume. We sat on mats and dined at tables abounding with island fruits, ferns, flowers, leis, and the inevitable soda pop bottles.

"The strolling Hawaiian musicians sang for the sheer joy of expressing happiness and thanksgiving. . . the spirit was contagious and *aloha* filled the air.

"Who can forget the impromptu, warm hospitality of an old plantation home. Fellowship centered around the kitchen table. From the ice box and stove came *sashimi* and beer, coffee and hot Portuguese bread, chop suey, or *Kanaka* stew and sour *poi*!

"It's known as Hawaiian Hospitality. . . that old Hawaiian way that blends east and west and flavors a meal with love at any table.

"In other words. . . 'The Island Way.' "

IN THE BEGINNING

Thanks to those original, restless natives who migrated from the south to settle in a new Polynesia, we still enjoy their first fruits. . . pig, chicken, *taro*, sweet potato, breadfruit, yam, banana, sugar cane, coconut, arrow root, and the *kukui* nut. They didn't need recipe books. . . they just combined a bit of this with that, and we're still using some of those original concoctions.

These Hawaiians were excellent farmers and fishermen, ingenious engineers in the *taro* patches, and master home and canoe builders. They fashioned needed utensils, weapons, and ornaments from stone, wood, or bone.

These natives lived close to nature in a mild climate. They simply didn't need the burden of much clothing. They took to the water like ducks, and babies were tossed in the ocean to learn to swim before they even walked. They had a healthy respect for the sea, which afforded both sport and sustenance. There was no lack of the latter. . . fish, *limu*, salt, and various sea creatures. If they couldn't eat up the day's catch, they traded it for fruit or other needed commodities with a neighbor or simply hung it up in the sun to dry for future use.

These people did not want for an abundance of wholesome foods, and maintained a diet high in minerals. Hawaiians were noted for their beautiful teeth, and it was a sign of beauty for women to be stout. The natives had only three condiments. . . *kukui, limu* and salt.

Taro was their main crop and considered a symbol of man's growth. As it still is today, *poi* was their rice, bread, and potatoes. Having no refrigeration didn't bother them at all. They just wrapped the poi in *ti* leaves, placed it in a wooden bowl and covered it with a layer of water and more *ti* leaves until ready to eat. At mealtime they removed what they needed and added more water for either one or two finger *poi*. Known for their hospitality, the Hawaiians ate from a single large calabash of poi at mealtime. Individual bowls would indicate stinginess or that a guest was not welcome!

The Hawaiians had their own system for boiling and cooking foods. After heating the stones over an open fire, they grabbed the red-hot stones and dropped them into a gourd filled with water. Presto! Instant boiling water. If it started to simmer instead of boil, all you had to do was reach for another red hot *pohaku*. However, most of the cooking was done by steaming underground, and we still use the same method today when we continue to cook in the *imu* or steam our food. They were wise cooks, too. . .very *akamai*. The Hawaiians loved to eat, and so they cooked enough food at one time to last for several days.

Pigs, chickens, fish, *taro*, potatoes, breadfruit, bananas, and yams were all placed over a bed of hot porous stones, covered with juicy banana tree trunks split in half, and *ti* and ginger leaves for flavor. Then the menu was covered with more leaves and old mats to keep the food clean and protected from the final covering of earth. Once the *imu* was closed, the food was left to steam for hours on end. . . and everyone went off to play. *Akamai!*

TODAY

'Tis said, "A man's home is his castle." And an old Chinese proverb aptly says: "A wife is honored more for her culinary skills than beauty. Beauty fades but a good cook improves with age."

So why not just relax and enjoy that aging process in a happy salon. . . your kitchen.

A workable kitchen needn't have all the modern appliances and fancy gadgets gathering dust and cluttering up precious counter space. An old refrigerator painted bright yellow alive with pictures of and by *moopunas,* post cards from travelling friends, cartoons and yellowed clipt recipes has far more personality than a pristine expensive panelled lab.

And if you're lucky enough to feature a round table with comfy chairs in the middle of your salon, maybe there's a lazy-susan in the middle. In grandma's day it held the sugar bowl of raw sugar, a can of cream, bottles of chili pepper water, Worcestershire and ketsup, jars of hard tack, guava jelly, and red salt. It was the hub of a wheel of happy living.

The table is also a happy spot to pore over week-end specials, ponder menus and dust off a few recipes to think about trying. Anyway, there's something here for all of us. So hopefully, you'll use and enjoy living 'The Island Way'.

Here's to the cook!

....Tips for K.P.....

TIPS FOR EASIER AND HAPPIER K.P.

Flowers or potted plants. . . a must around the house. Include them in your food budget. Their smiling faces and scent will lift many a weary soul.

The joys of an electric skillet and slow cooker are endless. Keep them within easy reach.

Keep an extra loaf or two of bread in the freezer for sandwiches or bread crumbs. Just whack off a wad of slices and grate.

A running supply of empty catsup, creme de menthe or wine bottles is just the thing to mix those packaged salad dressings in. Shake, use, store, and toss out.

Parmesan cheese. . . small, large or by the gross. . . never be without.

A box of biscuit mix is a cook's best friend. Anyone can follow directions and recipes on the box are ever changing.

Use frozen pie and pattie shells. . . who's to know!

Lime flavored gelatin is basic for aspics. . . don't run out, buy while they're on special.

Spare your guests the frustration of peeking through the floral arrangements on the dinner table. Keep your arrangements low and the candles glowing.

Warm the plates when food should be served hot, and chill them when it should be cold.

Scan the labels and wrappers on cans, boxes and jars. The best recipe for *Nuts and Bolts* is on a cereal box.

Never, never throw out those cottage cheese cartons or plastic oleo tubs. Clean and rinse well. They're perfect for transporting picnic-fare or freezing odds and ends.

If you buy rice in large quantities, add a bay leaf or two to keep the bugs away. Sprinkle cinnamon around and it supposedly keeps the silverfish away. Anyway, it smells nice.

Place forks, spoons, etc. in their own separate slots in the dishwasher bin. You can just grab them at one time and return to places in drawer with no sorting after they're clean.

You'll be wiser and happier making your stew a few days in advance and refrigerating it. It's then so easy to crack the top crust of grease and toss out. And think of all the calories you're missing!

Place tomatoes in a brown bag, set in corner of sink, make a cuff around the top, and pour in boiling water. The bag will split after a few seconds. . . and they will be ready to skin. Then all you need to do is slip them into a cellophane bag, place in refrigerator and they're ready to use at any time.

Don't forget!! If you feel someone deserves a compliment. . . take time out and tell him! Wouldn't you like to hear it!

And remember. . . a good cook cleans up after himself!

A QUICK REFERENCE WHEN IN DOUBT

3 teaspoons	1 tablespoon
2 tablespoons	1 liquid ounce
4 tablespoons	1/4 cup
16 tablespoons	1 cup
2 cups	1 pint
2 pints	1 quart
4 quarts	1 gallon
16 ounces	1 pound
2 cups solid butter	1 pound

Juice of 1 lemon	2-1/2 to 3-1/2 T
Juice of 1 orange	5 to 6 T

Can Size

8 ounce can	1 cup
No. 1 can	10-1/2 ounces, 1-1/4 cups
No. 2 can	1 pound 4 ounces, or 2-1/2 cups
No. 3-1/2 can	1 pound 13 ounces or 3-1/2 cups

For Reference
Small t stands for teaspoon
Big T stands for Tablespoon
C stands for cup
Aji = Ajinomoto or monosodium glutemate

...Drinks...

THIS ONE'S ON THE HOUSE - DRINKS

There comes a time when *Punch*. . . with or without. . . is the only answer; the Christmas festivities call for a special *Egg-Nog*; or hospitality demands an ever-ready pitcher of *Ice Tea*.

Here are the options. . .and one especially for the fair lady who coyly stammers . . . "A *Side-Car*, if it's not too much trouble, please."

ICE TEA

Ice Tea: Barely boil 3 qts. water and 1 1/3 C sugar, remove from fire and add either 2-3 T of instant tea mix or 1/2 C tea and steep five minutes then strain. Cool. Add 3/4 C fresh lemon juice and sprig of mint and keep that in your icebox! To serve add fresh sprigs of mint and long wedges of pineapple in tall glasses over ice.

ISLAND PUNCH

Island Punch: Mix cup to cup of fresh or frozen guava juice, surinam cherry juice, *lilikoi* and pineapple juice with water and sugar to taste and serve over ice with sprigs of fresh mint. Or substitute bottled soda for the water at the last minute.

PINEAPPLE TEMPTATION

Pineapple Temptation: In a large bowl let 1 pint of vanilla ice cream and 1 pint lemon sherbet soften slightly at room temperature. Add 2 C canned pineapple juice, 2 T lemon juice and 1 1/2 T grated lemon rind. Beat with egg beater or electric mixer at low speed until frothy. Add ginger ale; beat slightly until foamy. Serve in chilled glasses, garnished with rest of rind and mint.

HAWAIIAN PUNCH

Hawaiian Punch: In large punch bowl filled with cubes of ice and quart of lime or guava sherbet, pour 46 ounce can guava juice and 28 ounce bottle ginger ale and float sprigs of mint.

For a delightful cooler try mixing a glass of chilled root beer and a scoop of vanilla ice cream. Remember the *Root Beer Floats!* Ginger ale is good, too.

Or to a tall glass of chilled left-over coffee add a scoop of ice cream and cool off! Try it sometime after dinner with your sanka.

TOMATO JUICE

Tomato Juice cries for seasoning most of the time and with this you can really go overboard with the shakes and dashes. To a pitcher of tomato juice add a dash of marjoram, basil, thyme, tarragon, dill weed, savory and celery salt plus lemon juice, Worcestershire sauce or tabasco and anything else you like. . . it needs jazzing up.

VIRGIN MARY

For Virgin Mary serve plain with stalks of crisp celery or stalks of cucumber.

BLOODY MARY

For Bloody Mary serve with an ounce and a half of vodka or gin in old fashion glasses with lots of ice and the garbage if you like.

Ever tried the milk of the young coconut mixed with gin?

Or a *Saki Martini?*

A good stand-by for luncheons which can be made up in advance is a *Daquiri*. Just remember: 1 part fresh lemon or lime juice, 2 parts water and 3 parts rum, dark. Sweeten to taste before adding the rum. Serve over either finely crushed ice or just over the rocks. You can make pitchers full!

Remember when the *Side Car* was so popular! 1 part Cointreau, 3 parts brandy and 1 part lime juice. Simple.

FISH HOUSE PUNCH

Fish House Punch: In a punch bowl dissolve 1/4 pound sugar in 7 C tea. Add 3 T lemon juice and stir thoroughly. Blend in 3 C Jamaican rum, fifth of brandy, and a fifth of peach brandy. Carefully slip in a block of ice and ladle punch over ice to chill. *A little goes a long way!* The story goes that when George Washington imbibed, it was the only night there wasn't an entry in his diary!

VIRGIN ISLAND RUM PUNCH

Virgin Island Rum Punch: 1 pint rum, 1 pint prepared coffee, juice of 1 fat lime, dash of vanilla, little sugar. . . pour over crushed ice.

EGGNOG

Eggnog: Beat 12 egg yolks until thick and yellow, add 1 1/2 C sugar and beat again. Stir in 1 quart brandy and 1 pint rum slowly and then 1 1/2 quarts milk and 1 quart heavy cream. Just before serving fold in a dozen egg whites, stiffly beaten and serve very cold garnished with nutmeg. Your crystal punch cups are perfect for this.

THE VELVET HAMMER

The Velvet Hammer: Serve this one only in elegant stemmed crystal goblets. Could be listed under *Drinks* or *Dessert*. . . you decide.

In the blender pour in 1 1/2 ounces Cointreau, 1-1/2 ounces Cream de Cacao (light), 1 scoop vanilla ice cream and give it a whirl.

Double, triple, keep blending all evening if you like. For a change try green Creme de Menthe instead of Cacao.

Chill either champagne glasses or large

stemmed wine glasses, fill with several cubes of ice, add a twist of the rind and peel of fresh orange and pour chilled champagne over it.

PTY STRAWBERRIES AND
CHAMPAGNE PUNCH

PTY Strawberries and Champagne Punch: In a blender chop 2 pounds strawberries with the juice and outer skins of 2 lemons. Combine with 1 pint gin and 10 bottles of champagne at the last minute. Serve very cold!

Pupus

GRAB SOME BLOTTERS - PUPUS

Cocktails for two or twenty call for nuts, snacks, canapes, blotters, rabbit food or h'or d'ouvres. . . better known as *Pu-pus* to us! You can spend hours preparing elaborate molded pates and aspics or pull down a few jars, open a can of this and mix it with that, add a splash of whatever and surround the results with crackers. You're the hostess, it's up to you. . . send your guests limping to the nearest Drive-Inn or let them make a meal off of your scrumptious provisions.

Variety is the spice of life!

CHEESE WAFERS

Cheese Wafers: Add 1/4 t tabasco or Worcestershire sauce and a shake of cayenne pepper to 1/4 C butter and cream well. Blend in 3 ounces sharp cheddar cheese and 2/3 C flour sifted with 1/4 t salt. Mix, knead and form the mixture into rolls, wrap in wax paper and chill in refrig. Cut in 1/8 inch thick slices and place on cookie sheet to bake at 350 for 12-15 min-utes. Sprinkle paprika for decor before baking. Make and bake some now, freeze some and bake later. . . always handy!

CHEESE BALLS WITH SAUSAGE

Cheese Balls with Sausage: Add 10 ounces grated sharp cheese to 1 1/2 C Bisquick (the gal's best friend) and break in 1 pound hot sausage meat. Mix it all up well with your 'lily whites' and form into balls. Bake in 400 degree oven for 10 minutes. Keep hot to serve.

GREEN DUNK

Green Dunk: Your dieting friends will love you for this round.

Thaw 1 package frozen chopped spinach, squeeze out *all* moisture, mix with 1 large package non-fattening cream cheese, grated onion to taste, 1 6 1/2 ounce can minced clams and add only enough juice for dipping consistency. Add dash of lemon juice and whatever seasoning you prefer, mix thoroughly and chill. Set it midst a garden of colorful slices of green peppers, carrots, celery, radishes, zucchini, cauliflower, mushrooms, etc. etc. etc. Whatever is left over you can always throw in the stew pot.

CHICKEN LIVER PATE

Chicken Liver Pate: Cook in lots of butter 1 pound chicken livers and 1 big chopped onion in covered skillet. Then place it all in a blender with a *big* wedge of roquefort cheese and one large 16 ounce package cream cheese. Blend and add salt and pepper. . . and 2 jiggers brandy! Let it whirl! Chill to serve with toast squares or rounds.

SQUID AND MISO SAUCE

GRACE MORIMOTO whips this up automatically and admits she never measures just tastes! Her Sliced Squid and Miso Sauce is one of her best tastes.

Use either fresh or frozen squid, peel the skin, put it in pan and throw hot water over to swish it around, drain and slice in bite size pieces. *Miso Sauce*: grate thumb size piece of ginger, chop 2 small stalks green onions and combine with about 2 T miso, approximately 1 t of sugar, squeeze of lemon and 1 T vinegar and a dash of aji. . . or add or subtract to your 'taste'.

BONELESS CHICKEN BITS

JANE IBARA'S Boneless Chicken Bits are always a hit.

Debone and cut 2 pounds chicken thighs into chunk or bite-size pieces. Combine and thoroughly mix: 4 T mochiko flour (in Oriental food section of market), 4 T cornstarch, 4 T sugar, 1/2 t salt, 5 T soy, 1/2 t aji, 2 T chopped green onions, 2 slightly beaten eggs, 1 small clove garlic minced and small piece of ginger chopped fine (optional). Marinate chicken for at least 2 hours or longer, turning to coat, and fry in hot oil to brown and crispen. Serve hot garnished with parsley.

DRIED FISH

Dried Fish: Sprinkle split whole fish generously with Hawaiian rock salt (*Pa-a-kai*) and hang to dry in hot sun for day or two. If you have a screened box you can beat the flies. Keeps in covered jar for weeks and a good nibbler.

ROQUERFORT COGNAC DIP

Roquefort Cognac Dip: Mix together 1/2 pound roquefort cheese, crumbled, a cup of brandy and an 8-ounce package cream cheese and 1/2 C finely chopped macadamia nuts. Beat until smooth and fluffy. Serve with assorted crackers, toasted rye rounds or slices of tart apples or pears.

NIBBLERS

Nibblers: Mix together proportionally (we're heavy on the bugles). . . corn, wheat and rice chex, cheerios, thin pretzels, bugles and peanuts. Dribble over sufficient mixture of melted oleo, worcestershire sauce and garlic salt to coat well. Bake in slow oven about 3/4 hour stirring frequently. Jars don't last long and great for nibblers.

HOT CHEESE AND CRAB

JANE GROENENDYK says men love her special Hot Cheese and Crab. Mix together: 2 jars Kraft Old English cheese (5 ounces sharp or similar), 1 (6 ounce) can crab; 1/3 C sliced green onions; 6-8 drops tabasco. Pour into oven-proof casserole as you can serve right from the oven. Heat at 300 degrees for about 20 minutes or until everything is blended and cheese melted. Serve with crackers.

HOMEMADE CORN CHIPS

Or Homemade Corn Chips: In a mixing bowl thoroughly sift together 1 C cornmeal, 1/2 C flour, 3/4 t salt, 1/4 t baking soda. Add combined mixture of 1/2 C water, 3 T melted butter and 1/2 t or more tabasco sauce. Stir til dough forms a ball and knead on floured surface for about 5 minutes. Divide and roll out quite thin, sprinkle with salt, cut to your own dimensions. . . big, small, medium, thick or thin, up to you. . . and bake on cookie sheets at 350 until golden brown. . . 10-15 minutes. Cool and store.

CHEESE BALLS

ELLEN TOWNSLEY'S Cheese Balls are deliteful little surprises. Blend 1/2 pound sharp cheddar cheese, grated, with 1/2 C butter, add 1 C flour, 1 t salt and dash of Worcestershire. Wrap small amounts around either stuffed green olives or button mushrooms and form into balls. Place on cookie sheet to freeze and keep frozen in plastic bags for use any time. Bake 425 oven for 12 minutes and serve hot.

BROILED ONION ROUNDS

Broiled Onion Rounds: Cut slices of bread into rounds and brown on one side slitely under oven broiler. Chop, chop, chop one medium onion as fine as you can and wrap in several paper towels once, twice, three times and again to remove all juice. Combine for spreading consistency with shakes of Parmesan cheese, mayonnaise, salt and pepper and dash of tabasco. Pile on untoasted side of rounds and broil to bubble and brown slitely. Keep hot and serve.

KIM CHEE DIP

SUE LITTLEJOHN recommends making a lot of this dip as it disappears like magic! Kim Chee Dip: In blender chop 1/2 jar Kim Chee and about 2 drops of juice. . . don't want it runny. Blend in 2 8-ounce packages cream cheese and one heaping T mayonnaise to right consistency for dipping potato chips or spreading on crackers.

EGGPLANT CAVIAR

Eggplant Caviar: Bake 1 large eggplant (about an hour in 400 oven), remove skin and chop pulp. In skillet heat 4 T olive oil with a clove of garlic (remove when brown), 1 large onion chopped fine, 1/4 C chopped parsely, 2 T either sherry or tarragon vinegar, add salt and pepper to taste and eggplant pulp. Cook, stirring constantly until thickened. . . about 15 minutes. Re-check for taste. Cool, chill thoroughly and serve with corn chips, crackers or melba toast.

QUICK AVOCADO SPREAD

Avocados a drug on the market? Make and freeze some dip.

Quick Avocado Spread: Combine 4 avocados, mashed or pureed, 1 package (1 3/8 ounces) onion soup mix, 2 T lemon juice and

1/2 C sour cream. Mix well, cover and chill. Makes about 3 1/2 cups.

AVOCADO BALLS

Or you may simply serve Avocado Balls. Use your melon ball scoop to form little balls, spray with lemon juice, pierce with toothpics and serve with following *Sauce*: Combine chili sauce, lemon juice and tabasco to taste.

STUFFED EGG

The Stuffed Egg platter always needs re-filling. Use the small size eggs. . . they're easier to pop. Hard boil your eggs, drain, run under cold water and then shell. Cut in half, scoop out the yolk and mash well. Add: chopped chives, horseradish-mustard, dash of thyme and salt and pepper and mix up with mayonnaise to blend. Fill the whites with mixture and garnish with small sprigs of fresh parsely and sprinkle with paprika. A caviar topping is good, too.

For an alternative: to the mashed yolk add curry powder, dashes of ginger powder, garlic salt, grated onion to taste and mayonnaise to blend.

QUICHE LORRAINE

Quiche Lorraine can be prepared ahead of time and kept frozen. If frozen cook at 450 degrees for 30 minutes. For one big pan or three small ones. *Crust:* 4 C flour, 1 t salt, 1 1/4 C butter (2 1/2 blocks), 2 eggs, 1/2 C water. Mix, roll out and lay crust in pan or pans and put in icebox for one hour. Then pour in the following *Filling:* 12 ounces chopped Swiss cheese, 16 ounces chopped ham, 1 large and 1 small can of evaporated milk, 2 t salt, 6 eggs, 1/2 t nutmeg and 1 t pepper. Bake in 350 oven for 45 minutes. Cut to bite-size and serve hot or cold. A french favorite of MARGARET COMMUNIEUX.

CRISP WON TON

Crisp Won Ton: 1 10-ounce package of Won Ton Pi (moist) wrappers makes about 45. Fry 1 pound ground pork until cooked, add: 1/2 pound raw fish cake, 1/2 C minced water chestnuts, 1/4 C finely minced ham, 3/4 C finely chopped green onions, 1/4 C finely chopped Chinese parsley, 1 t each soy, aji, salt and sugar and 1 unbeaten egg. Continue cooking briefly then leave to cool. Drop teaspoons of mixture on squares, moisten edge of wrapper with water and press firmly together to close securely. Deep fry in hot oil, turning once until brown, drain on paper towel and serve hot. Can be frozen well, too. Serve with soy and hot mustard sauce according to taste.

CHIPPED BEEF PUPU

And BEE FRELINGHUYSEN'S Chipped Beef Pupu is easy, different, elegant and keeps indefinitely. Blend together 1 (8-ounce) package cream cheese, 2 T milk, 1 (2 1/2-ounce) jar chipped beef (chopped in blender), 2 T minced onion or onion soup mix, 1/2 C sour cream. Smooth into 8-inch pie tin or an oven-proof dish suitable for serving directly from oven. Sprinkle top with 2 T minced green pepper and 1/4 C coarsely chopped walnuts (or macs). Bake 350 oven for 15 minutes, cool, serve with biscuits or crackers or dip in with potato chips.

Need something in a hurry! Combine chunky peanut butter with finely chopped mango chutney and some juice. Spread on crackers or fill stalks of celery.

Remember. . . your hungry cocktail guests will love you if you have a platter of dainty sandwiches circulating. See them under *Sandwiches*, especially, the watercress and the corn beef ones.

Here are two Island favorites to be found in the pamphlets the ladies of the *Pacific Tropical Botanical Garden* put out.

TARO CHIPS RECIPE I

Taro Chips Recipe I: Peel raw *taro* corms and slice thin with slicer. Deep fry in oil heated to 380 degrees. Drain on paper towels and salt generously. These may be frozen for later use.

RECIPE II

Recipe II: Boil whole unpeeled taro til cooked through. Chill. Then slice as thin as possible. Fry in hot oil until crisp, about 10 minutes. Use frying pan or deep fryer. Drain on cake rack, absorbent paper and sprinkle with salt or garlic salt. Can be frozen.

BREADFRUIT CHIPS

Breadfruit Chips: Cut a scrubbed raw green breadfruit in quarters or sixths. Peel and remove large core. Put in a bowl with ice cubes and refrigerate until thoroughly chilled (overnight). Then slice as thin as possible. . . the thinner the better. . . and return to the ice water.

Heat oil in deep fryer to 395. Quickly dry a few slices at a time and drop into the hot oil.

Fry until golden brown, drain on absorbent paper, and salt immediately. Store in airtight containers in refrigerator or freeze.

PROSCIUTTO MANGOES

DOTTIE KANEAIAKALA gathered the last three mangoes from her Hayden mango tree and invented Prosciutto Mangoes. "You don't have to have Italian ham", said Dottie. "I just cooked a Farmer John, sliced it real thin, made alternating slices of mango, a grinding of coarse black pepper, ham and chilled. Presto Prosciutto!"

CHEESE DIP

NETTY HANSEN'S Cheese Dip is fabulous and can be made ahead of time and frozen.

Into the top of a double boiler cut 1 pound each sharp cheddar cheese and Velveeta cheese into cubes and melt. Then add the following ingredients and cook for about 45 minutes or an hour: 2 small onions grated, 1 clove garlic minced (or powdered), 2 green chili peppers (canned and wash out seeds and dice), ajinomoto, drops of tabasco or Worcestershire, and 1/2 a Portuguese sausage sliced.

Use the large size corn chips to dip into this treat.

PUPU PLATTER

TERRI SCOTT had one of the prettiest and most tempting pupu arrangements. On an ample platter were arranged: 1 gigantic green pepper, topped and de-seeded and filled with a single but subtle mix of 1/2 mayonnaise,

1/2 sour cream with tabasco, Worcestershire and curry to taste.

Beside this was snuggled a smallish red cabbage which she had topped and dug out some innards with a sharp knife leaving just enough room to place a glass dish holding the dip. Combine 1/2 sour cream, 1/2 mayonnaise and to taste add at least 1 t dill weed, lemon juice, Beaumonde, Worcestershire, cayenne and celery salt. . . correct seasoning.

Standing beside these were two fat cucumbers one taller than the other, which had been cut to stand, de-seeded and used to hold stalks of green onions and young celery stalks.

Surrounding this bevy of garden beauties were flowerettes of cauliflower, radish roses, strips of chop suey yams, bell pepper sticks, rounds of zucchini, sliced fresh mushrooms and carrot sticks.

Terry said she couldn't find an extra large onion otherwise she would have used it, too, by cutting off the top and removing all but the two fattest outside layers and using it as a natural bowl to hold sweet gerkins.

BEEF JERKY

For those who like it hot try ALICE CHING'S Beef Jerky. Cut 2 pounds of flank steak into 2 1/2 inch strips. Soak for 2 days in following marinade: 1 C soy, 4 T sugar, 2 T each ajinomoto, sherry, sesame seed, 2 cloves garlic, and 1 package Kim Chee paste or mix.

Bake on wire rack at 200 for 3 hours. Turn meat over after baking for 1 1/2 hours. Slice and fry in lightly greased pan to serve hot.

TARO-PORK PUPU

Taro-Pork Pupu: Use up your left-over oven-kalua pig by shredding it in smallish pieces and add a bit more liquid smoke and an ample sprinkle of red salt.

Combine this with mashed fresh *taro* that has been cooked until quite soft. Add some mochiko flour (Oriental department) to hold it together, along with just a bit of butter as the pork may not be fatty enough. Mash and blend the combination well, form into little balls and bake in 350 oven 10 minutes. Let it pull together a few minutes before serving.

EGGPLANT CAVIAR

Combine Eggplant Caviar with equal portions of mashed avocado, dash of tabasco and serve with corn chips.

OIO TEMPURA

Oio Tempura by HINAYO HAMAMOTO won a prize at the local food fair. Cook 1 *gobo* scraped, 2 small carrots chopped, 6 water chestnuts chopped, and 3 dried mushrooms sliced with a little salt, soy and sugar for a short while.

Combine cooked mixture with 2 C scraped oio, 2 T salt, 4 T sugar, 1 C cornstarch, 2 eggs beaten, 3 C water, 2 stalks green onions slivered, rind of 1/2 an orange grated, 2 t ginger cut up small or grated, 4 leaves of chico (imported from Japan) chopped.

Mix well and drop by spoonfuls into hot oil and cook tempura style until golden brown.

MAKI SUSHI

GLADYS HORNER'S Maki Sushi is another winner. Wash 7 cups raw rice, add 2 T salt with 7 C water. Gladys says that today the rice seems to spoil fast and is less absorbent so you may need 1/2 or 1/4 C more water, depending on the rice brand.

Pour all the cooked rice in a large bowl and stir in 1 C sugar, 3/4 C rice vinegar and 2 t ajinomoto. Mix well and let cool.

Spread about 1/2 C of rice over sheet of nori (seaweed) evenly and lay on the following ingredients: 4 scrambled eggs fried and sliced 1/4 or 1/2 inch strips the length of the nori; 1 can tuna heated with 3 T sugar and 2 T soy; slices of *daikon*, sprinkle green and red powdered shrimp over all. Roll up and moisten end of nori with vinegar or water to seal securely. Makes 20-22 rolls.

You may add more filler such as fish cake, mushrooms, sausage, carrots, stringbeans. . . precooked and flavored before adding on top of the rice.

HOT TOMATO SAUCE DIP

JUNE SEKIOKA'S Hot Tomato Sauce Dip is great for serving with corn ships as pupus or you may also use this as sauce for tacos.

Combine and cook for 1 hour: 2 large cans whole tomatoes, mashed, 1 large chopped onion, 2 pieces chopped garlic, 1 t cumin, ground or seed, 1/2 t oregano, 2 t salt, 4 T sugar, 2 t Worcestershire sauce, 2 (10 ounce) cans ortega (tomatoes and hot green chili) and 1/4 t ajinomoto.

Simmer additional 2 to 2 1/2 hours without cover until thick. Refrigerate.

SARAH WILDER was the first person to bring the art of creative pottery to Hawaii in 1930. Her fame as a great hostess was due to the fact she was born a gourmet cook and insisted on preparing every bit of food for her many original parties.

CAMEMBERT EN CAPTIVITE

Camembert En Captivite means just what it says and Sarah's guests loved ferreting it out.

Boil up 2 tins of undiluted consomme with a stalk of celery, sprigs of parsley and small onion all chopped and allspice to flavor. Soak 2 packages gelatin in 1/2 C water to soften. Strain consomme, add 1 T each tarragon vinegar and Worcestershire sauce and combine with gelatin. Pour half in rather deep dish and place in icebox to jell.

When just beginning to harden, lay round of Camembert on it and add the rest of gelatin mixture. Leave overnight, release by setting in hot water very briefly and turn on pretty dish and surround with crackers.

CRUNCHY CHEESE PUFFS

STEPHANIE ELLIS'S Crunchy Cheese Puffs make 4 dozen pupus. Beat 1/2 C soft butter until fluffy, mix in 2 C shredded sharp cheddar cheese, 1/2 t Worcestershire sauce and a dash of cayenne. Add 1 C sifted all-purpose flour and blend thoroughly. Chill dough for several hours.

Shape into 1-inch balls, roll in coarsely crushed chow mein noodles and place on ungreased baking sheet. Bake in pre-heated 350 oven for 12 to 15 minutes or until golden brown. Serve hot.

HOT CLAM AND CHEESE DIP

CHIYONO TAKEMOTO puts a new twist on the ole favorite clam dip. . . Hot Clam and Cheese Dip. Melt 3 T butter and brown 1 small onion finely chopped and 1/2 green pepper finely chopped. Then add: 1 C minced clams, drained, 1/4 pound processed cheese, cut in small pieces, 4 T catsup, 1 T Worcestershire sauce, 1 t sherry and 1/4 t cayenne pepper. Cook until cheese melts and try to keep it warm while serving with crackers or cocktail rye bread.

SALMON DIP

ADELAIDE JACINTHO'S Salmon Dip: Drain 1 1-pound can of salmon and mash. Blend in 1/2 t salt, 3 dashes tabasco, and 1 t grated onion. Add 1 C sour cream and cover to chill thoroughly. Serve with crackers or chips.

SPINACH DIP

Hale Kea Spinach Dip for fresh Waimea veggies: Cook 1 package frozen chopped spinach and drain off all excess liquid.

In bowl mix 1 C sour cream, 1/2 C mayonnaise, 1 C minced fresh parsley, 1/2 C minced scallions, 1/2 t Beau Monde, 1/2 t dried dill weed and salt and pepper to taste. Mix well. Add spinach and stir thoroughly. Check seasoning and chill well. Serve with fresh vegetables.

CHILI CHEESE CUBES

STEPHANIE ELLIS'S Chili Cheese Cubes can be served hot or cold. In a large bowl, beat 8 eggs until light and fluffy (about 5 minutes). Add 1/2 C flour, 1 t baking powder, and 1 t salt. Mix well.

Fold in 1 1/2 C each shredded Cheddar cheese, cottage cheese and shredded Monterey Jack cheese and 1 8-ounce can mild green chilis, drained, seeded and chopped. Turn into greased 9x9x13 inch baking dish and bake in 350 oven for 45 minutes. Cool and cut into small squares.

CHEESE PATE

Cheese Pate can be made ahead. Sprinkle 1 t gelatin over 1 C hot consomme and stir to dissolve. Combine it with 2-3 cloves of minced garlic, 1 8-ounce bar of softened cream cheese, a few shakes of Worcestershire and blend until smooth. Chill until firm and serve with crackers.

QUICK DIP

Quick Dip for vegetables or crackers. Combine 1 C small curd cottage cheese with 2 t curry, 1 t instant chicken bouillon, 1/4 t seasoned salt and 1 T dried parsley. Blend well, chill and serve.

MUSHROOM ROLLS

Something very snappy is Mushroom Rolls: Saute 1/2 pound fresh, finely chopped mushrooms in 1/4 C butter for about 5 minutes. Blend in 3 T flour, 2 t salt, 1/2 t Accent and gradually stir in 1/2 C light cream. Keep stirring and cook until thickened. Add 2 T minced chives, 1 T lemon juice, and cool.

Remove crusts from 25 slices of extra thin sliced white bread, roll each slice lightly with rolling pin, and spread with mixture. Roll up. To serve cut each roll in half or thirds and place under broiler to toast. Serve hot.

HAMBURGER SAUSAGE

Hamburger Sausage makes great pupus served with sliced cheese, and a batch in the freezer is always handy, too. To 1 pound good, lean ground round add 1 T each curing salt and cumin, 1 t each garlic and onion salt, 1 T liquid smoke and ground pepper to taste. If you like it hot, add either chili powder, home-made chili pepper water or hot pepper sauce to taste.

Combine ingredients and mix well. Shape into rolls about 2 inches in diameter, wrap in aluminum foil and refrigerate 24 hours. Remove from foil and roll up tightly in nylon net, secure ends and bake in 325 oven for 2 hours.

PECAN GALA DIP

MARILYN GOSS serves this Pecan Gala Dip hot and bubbly with corn chips and guests forget their diets! Combine 1 softened 8-ounce package cream cheese with 2 T milk and blend well. Stir in 2-1/2 ounce jar dried chipped beef, 1/4 C finely chopped green pepper, 1/2 T garlic flakes, 1/4 t pepper, and fold in 1/2 C sour cream. Spoon into shallow baking dish. Heat 2 T butter and crispen 1/2 C coarsley chopped pecans and sprinkle over mixture. Bake in 350 oven for 20 minutes.

_____. . . *PUPUS*

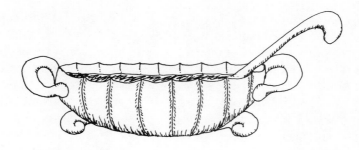

....Soups....

SOME LIKE IT HOT SOME LIKE IT COLD SOUPS

Remember the days when there was always a big pot of soup simmering on the back burner. . . the kitchen smelled heavenly, Dad had a spot to revive him after a grueling day, and sometimes the family made a nutritious and filling meal of it.

Any fowl carcass, leg bone, or soup bones plus left overs and chopped veggies with lots of imagination with herbs and seasonings can simmer down to a real pottage without much trouble. Season hi, season low. . . all to taste after the basics.

Remember the basic rule of a good bowl of soup. . . hot soup means steaming and chilled soup means absolutely icy cold, and this includes the bowls, too!

ONE OF EACH SOUP

One of Each Soup you have to try to believe! One medium size potato, onion, apple, banana, and one celery heart leaves and all is the start. Peel and roughly chop. Simmer in 1 pint chicken stock with 1 t salt until soft. Puree this and stir in 1 C light cream, 1 T melted butter, 1 t curry powder or more, pepper to taste. Do not cook longer. Cool and chill thoroughly. Sprinkle with chopped chives. Serve very, very cold or very very hot. . . either way is delicious.

AVOCADO-WATERCRESS SOUP

Avocado-Watercress Soup: In the blender toss in 1 small onion chopped, 1/2 bunch chopped and cleaned watercress stems and leaves, 2 sliced avocados, 1 can consomme, 1 T lime juice, garlic salt, pepper and tabasco for zing. Let it whirl. When nicely chopped and blended add a carton of sour cream and whir again briefly. Whisk into refrig to chill icy cold. Garnish with sprigs of watercress and dash of paprika.

OXTAIL SOUP

Oxtail Soup is ALEX KAAUA'S specialty and she loves it because the whole family gets in the act shelling peanuts! Brown 1 package oxtail in little oil, drain and add water to cover.

Add minced garlic, chopped and sliced ginger, skin and all for better taste, and simmer 3 hours. Add sliced *daikon*, 1/2 pound shelled raw peanuts, sliced carrots, salt, and aji to taste. Add 2 ounces sherry or bourbon and thicken with cornstarch if you wish. Serve in the old fashioned Chinese soup bowls with Chinese soup ladles. Have lots of hot rice available along with platters of grated *daikon*, chopped green onions, Chinese parsley, and chili pepper water.

SPINACH OYSTER SOUP

ANITA STUCKY has put together all her favorite family recipes in a beautiful loose leaf book for each of her children. . . something all of us yearn to do! Here's her Spinach Oyster Soup. Blend 3 jars baby food creamed spinach and 1 or 2 C drained oysters til smooth. Add 1 pint half-and-half cream and blend on low. Heat over low heat. . . *Do not boil*. . . put a dollop of cool whip on top to serve and sprinkle with nutmeg.

CHOOK

Chook: In a big pot throw in the turkey carcass and any left overs and a small island pork bone just for essence. Cover with water, add 1 large round onion sliced or diced and several fingers (more the merrier) of sliced ginger. Let this simmer on the back of the stove for as long as 8 hours. Drain off liquid, cool and remove meat from bones. Return stock and meat to pot. Add 1 C rice to 7 C stock (soak rice in water for at least an hour first). Let this simmer on the lowest heat. . . crockpot is great. . . for several hours or until the rice has cooked down to a gruel consistency.

But check and keep stirring occasionally as it does tend to stick. Season with Hawaiian salt and pepper to taste. You may add canned bits of mushrooms and sliced dry-soaked mushrooms, chopped water chestnuts, and more turkey or slivers of ham.

Serve piping hot and garnish with sprigs of Chinese parsley and sliced red pork with shredded lettuce and chopped green onions optional. A meal in itself and can be frozen very well.

WATERCRESS SOUP

Watercress Soup: Wash a fresh bunch of watercress well and rinse. Chop for blender and add 2 cans cream of mushroom soup and a 'breath' of grated onion. Depending on preference add 2 jars of table avoset or 1 jar and 1 C milk. Flavor gently with tabasco and Worcestershire, t powdered mustard and 2 or more t curry. Optional on the horseradish. Give it a good whirl in the blender until the watercress is really chopped and a beautiful green color. Chill.

With a dollop of whipped cream, sprig of parsley and paprika, you've got it! Be sure your bowls are pretty and *Cold.* If you have Celadon green ones or Rose Medallion sitting on the shelf. . . use them. It will not only look elegant but taste it, too. Excellent to serve between cocktails and the buffet table.

QUICK BORSCHT

Quick Borscht: Cook until tender 6 large beets, peel and dice while still hot and toss into blender with 3 cubes of chicken bouillon and 2 C hot water to blend. Add juice of a big lemon or vinegar equivalent, pinch of Hawaiian salt, small (very small) amount of grated onion just for zip, dill weed, pepper and onion salt. Turn to chop, then to puree and let it really blend. If too thick add a little more hot water and another cube of bouillon. This makes a quart and keeps in the refrig for several days. Good diet lunch with plain yogurt or with sour cream and dash of caviar for elegant dinner.

CHILLED TOMATO SOUP

Chilled Tomato Soup: In the blender combine 4 large ripe peeled tomatoes, 4 T ice water, 1 T sugar, 1 sliced white onion and puree nicely. You may or may not strain before adding 1 C sour cream. Refrigerate. Just before serving stir in 1 t grated lemon rind and 2 t lemon juice and stir well. Garnish with dollop of sour cream and sprig of parsley or chopped chives.

FISH CHOWDER

The all-time favorite Fish Chowder goes well with saloon pilots and a green salad. Fry 2 thinly sliced pork chops until cooked (10 minutes). Or fry up lots of sliced bacon, add chopped onions according to preference and simmer gently. Add dash of dill, majoram, parsley, salt and pepper. In a separate pot simmer fillets of any white fish, frozen *mahimahi* is good, too, but skin it first. Remove from stock and break into small pieces. Then add enough stock to pork and onions to simmer coarsely grated potatoes until cooked and the mixture thickens. . . keep stirring occasionally. Then add half and half or plain milk (but do use *some cream*) to the desired consistency and add fish

pieces. Check seasoning. Simmer gently to blend flavors. Serve piping hot and sprinkle freshly chopped parsley or chives over. Be sure you've made enough! A big pot of this chowder does wonders at a cocktail party!

GAZPACHO

MAGGIE COMMUNIEUX'S Gazpacho, a Spanish cold soup, can be made ahead of time and frozen, too. Into the blender put: 1 C chicken broth, 4 C canned tomato, 1-1/2 cucumber, 1-1/2 green pepper, 1 or 2 cloves of garlic and put on medium speed til all is blended smoothly. Then blend in another cup of broth, 1/2 C lemon juice, 1/4 C olive oil and salt and pepper. Let stand in refrigerator for at least 3 hours and serve well chilled. Makes 4-5 servings.

CHICKEN CURRY SOUP

This Chicken Curry Soup is one of the main attractions served at the Garden Cafe. In 3 quart saucepan saute until soft: 3 C chopped onion, 4 cloves minced garlic, 3 T each butter and Italian olive oil, 1-1/2 to 2 t curry powder from a freshly opened jar. Put all in blender and whirl until completely blended. Add to this mixture and blend until smooth: 2 cans condensed cream of potato soup (10-3/4 ounces), 2 C clear chicken broth, 2 C sour cream, 1/4 to 1/2 t Garden Cafe Spice or your own seasoning.

Return all to original pan and heat slowly until mixture thickens on sides of pan and flavors are blended, stirring often. Garnish with parsley, peanuts or a dollop of sour cream with a bit of good mango chutney on top. May also serve chilled. Garden Cafe Spice is available at the Garden Cafe.

SPLIT PEA SOUP

Another meal-in-one is a good Split Pea Soup. Cover either a left-over ham bone or ham hocks with water in large pot. . . use two packages of the frozen for lots of meat. Add chopped onions, carrots, celery, potatoes, bay leaf, salt and pepper and let simmer for an hour then add package of well rinsed green split peas. Continue cooking but be sure you watch the pot and stir occasionally so it doesn't stick. This will cook down to a good puree, the meat will fall off the bones in pieces and then you may remove any bones and either toss out or chop up the rind and return to soup. It tends to thicken when in the refrig for several days so just add a bit of water to start it bubbling again.

TOMATO BISQUE

JANE GROENENDYKE'S recipe for her Tomato Bisque tastes as tho she'd spent hours preparing it. Combine 2 cans tomato soup, 1 can beef bouillon, 1 small can Ortega, green chili salsa, and mix well. Leave in refrigerator to really chill.

Serve in cold soup bowls and sprinkle generously with grated cucumbers and hard boiled eggs. Garnish with sprigs of parsley.

LUNCHEON SOUP

MARION KEAT'S Favorite Luncheon Soup is simple, outrageously gourmet-tasting and baffling. Empty contents of one can of pea soup into saucepan and mix with another can of water. Add curry powder (about 1 T or to taste) to blend and pour in 1 can consomme.

Stir and blend until smooth, season to taste with salt and pepper and serve hot in soup cups. Float a thin slice of lemon on top and serve with toasted cheese sandwiches.

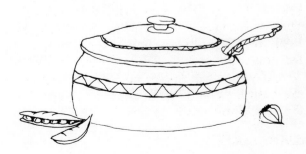

Salads

THE TEARIN' OF THE GREENS SALADS

For every season there is a salad and for any reason there is a salad! Lucky the person who has a vegetable and herb garden outside his back door. For top salads the greens must be fresh, crisp, clean and thoroughly rinsed and dried. Most popular raw greens are watercress, endive, romaine, spinach leaves, Chinese cabbage, red or white cabbage, iceberg lettuce and chicory. A good way to store lettuce after thoroughly rinsing and removing bad leaves is to shake well to remove excess water and store in covered plastic container lined with paper towel. This way you may just reach in to use. There are fancy draw-stringed bags made of huck toweling you may buy at specialty shops but you could whip one up yourself, too.

If you're salad-oriented never be without the basic lime and lemon flavored gelatins or the plain familiar orange box from Mr. Knox.

GINGER SLAW

BOB GAHRAN'S Ginger Slaw is a natural for ham. Shred a medium size firm head of cabbage with a sharp knife. Combine with the following dressing: 3/4 C mayonnaise, 2 or 3 T lemon or lime juice and 2 or 3 heaping T freshly grated ginger root (or 1 T dried ginger). Mix and toss thoroughly, turn into large bowl and sprinkle with paprika. Serves 6.

CORNED BEEF SALAD

SYBIL DEAN'S Corned Beef Salad is a great luncheon dish. Dissolve 1 envelope lemon flavored gelatin in 1 C hot water. As it starts to congeal whip in 1-3/4 C Miracle Whip (gotta be!) until foamy then dump in 1 12-ounce can corn beef broken in pieces, 3 chopped hard boiled eggs, 1 C diced celery, small amounts diced onion and green pepper and 1 small can pimiento chopped. Refrigerate. Serve on crisp lettuce. Serves 6.

MOLDED SHRIMP SALAD

ANITA STUCKY'S Molded Shrimp Salad: Soften 2 T unflavored gelatin in 1/2 C cold water, add to 1 C hot tomato soup and crumble in 1 8-ounce package soft cream cheese to melt and blend. Add 2 T milk, 1 C finely diced celery, 1/3 C finely diced green pepper, 1/2 C finely diced onion, and 1 C diced cooked shrimp (or tuna) and 1 C mayonnaise with a pinch of salt. Pour into greased mold and chill for 24 hours.

ARTICHOKE SALAD

Artichoke Salad: Rinse and trim prickly artichoke leaves so top is flat. Boil slowly in water to cover with dollop of olive oil, bay leaf, salt and ground pepper, one lemon squeezed and dropped in, or jigger of vinegar, sliced onion, sliced garlic cloves according to taste. When fork pierces bottom easily, drain and turn upside down to cool.

Pull out hairy center leaving heart exposed. Carefully spoon in *Shrimp Salad*. . . mix shrimps, dash of lemon juice so's not to be runny, shake of dill, salt and pepper and mayonnaise to hold it together. Garnish with paprika and sprigs of parsley. Chill well before serving. If you prefer you may use chicken, turkey or crab chopped with a bit of green onion, too.

RASPBERRY APPLESAUCE MOLD

Raspberry Applesauce Mold is good for holiday bird time. Bring to a boil; 1/4 C sugar, 1 C orange juice, 6 T lemon juice, 1 C shredded pineapple, 1 C pineapple juice, 1 (16 ounce) can raspberry applesauce and pinch of salt. Dissolve 2 packages raspberry flavored gelatin into the mixture. Stir well and add 1/2 C chopped walnuts and 2 small packages of creamed cheese broken into small chunks. When cheese is melted and blended with the other ingredients pour into mold and chill to set. Serve on bed of lettuce.

CHICKEN SALAD

Chicken Salad: Steam a roaster very gently and when cooked, de-bone, de-skin, de-vein, de-gristle and remove any fat. Dice for bite size pieces. In large bowl add to chicken bits: chopped celery, can of chopped water chestnuts, bell peppers, lots of parsley, chopped hard boiled eggs, and if you desire chopped green onions or watercress. Mix it all up with your favorite seasonings and lots of mayonnaise and serve very cold. Marinated artichoke hearts, pickled beets and tomato wedges add to the attraction, too.

Or you may want to use this to fill half a papaya or avocado or even an artichoke.

CHILI RING

Chili Ring: Dissolve 2 T gelatin in 1/2 C cold water. Heat 1 C chili sauce, 1 C mayonnaise, 1 C cottage cheese and combine with gelatin and 1 C whipping cream. Pour in bowl or mold to chill and set. Add this to the chicken salad menu or a bowl of marinated shrimps.

OLD FASHIONED POTATO SALAD

Old Fashioned Potato Salad is still the star picnic attraction and you can start it ahead of time, too. Day before wash and boil up some salad potatoes and throw in the eggs to hard boil the first 25 minutes after it starts boiling. Watch potatoes so they don't overcook and become mushy and fall apart! While still hot, peel and dice into bite-size pieces. Put in large bowl and douse with salad oil, vinegar or pickle juice, dash of celery and dill seed, salt and pepper, cover and refrigerate overnite.

Next day you can add as much as you like

of the basics: chopped celery, parsley, the boiled eggs, and *lots* of mayonnaise (the potatoes seem to absorb it).

The options are yours on: tuna, peas, slivered radishes, grated carrots, sliced green pepper, chopped onion (green for color), crisp bacon bits and even some elbow macaroni. For best tossing and marinating wash your 'lily-whites' thoroughly and mix the mayonnaise into the mixture lovingly and quickly. To serve, pack down on platter, surround with crisp, dry lettuce, sliced tomatoes, and garnish with parsley sprigs, sliced hard boiled eggs and paprika. Any cold ham around?

GLAZED CHICKEN PIECES

Glazed Chicken Pieces are elegant but simple to make, really. Carefully de-bone 2 pound box chicken thighs and simmer gently in water to cover (bones, too), sliced onion, 1/2 t celery seed, T minced parsley, bay leaf, dash of rosemary, dill seed and salt. When cooked, cool and remove skin. Make a glaze of the following: dissolve 2 envelopes unflavored gelatin in 1/2 C water over low heat and add one C mayonnaise. Dip pieces of chicken in mixture to cover and coat evenly. Chill until set. Have some fun. . . dress the pieces up with carrot slivers, parsley, green or ripe olives. . . or make funny faces using raisins for eyes!

TOMATO ASPIC

Don't throw away the stock! Make a Tomato Aspic. Drain, skim off fat by chilling and combine 1 C with 1 C stewed tomatoes muddled around, juice of half a lemon or 2 T vinegar, 1 T brown sugar, Worcestershire sauce,

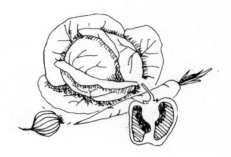

salt and pepper. Taste for any additional seasoning. Bring this to a rolling boil, and add a 3-ounce package lime flavored gelatin and pour into greased salad mold. To serve, fill center with cottage cheese and space the glazed chicken pieces around it on a bed of crisp lettuce. Add some stuffed eggs, canned asparagus and baby beets and you'll have a fancy luncheon on one platter!

NAMASU

Namasu: Partly peel the cucumber by running fork tines down the outside then slice very thin. Sprinkle with Hawaiian salt and let stand an hour. Squeeze out the slices and add to mixture of 1 t mashed ginger, 2 T sugar, 1/2 C vinegar, dash of aji. For color and vitamins add thin slivers of carrot.

SALMON MOUSSE

Salmon Mousse: De-bone and remove black skin from one large can red salmon, put in blender and add to taste: grated onion (about 2 t or 2 stalks chopped green onions), 1 T lemon juice, and if you like, several shakes of liquid Barbecue Smoke Sauce. Test flavoring.

Add 1 carton sour cream, 1 C mayonnaise, Worcestershire and blend it well. Dissolve 1 envelope unflavored gelatin slowly in 1/4 C water over low heat and add this to mix thoroughly. Season with dill, salt and fresh ground pepper. Mix well and turn into bowl or salad mold. Chill to set. Garnish with crisp watercress, cucumber slices, stuffed eggs and artichoke hearts.

A dressing of mayonnaise mixed with lots of lemon juice and dill will complement the fish.

Or chop up crisp, dry watercress and combine with mayonnaise and add tabasco or Worcestershire sauce.

Go the pupu route with the mousse too. Serve in bowl surrounded by thick slices of zucchini or cucumber.

LEMON COTTAGE CHEESE SALAD MOLD

Lemon Cottage Cheese Salad Mold: Dissolve 1 package lemon flavored gelatin in 1 C hot water and add: 1 C mayonnaise, 1 pint cottage cheese and cool. Then add 1/2 C chopped celery, 1 large cucumber diced, and 1 small onion grated, 1 t salt and 1 T vinegar. Combine well and chill to set in fancy bowl or ring.

If you want to hassle with the unmoulding process pour it into a fancy fish mould and serve with a bowl of marinated shrimps.

PICKLED ASPARAGUS

Pickled Asparagus from the book NANCY HEWITT wrote on all you want to know about the spear. Heat together: 1/2 C cider vinegar, 1/2 C red wine, 4 green onions chopped, 4 peppercorns, 1/2 t dill seed and 1/4 t salt. When hot pour over 1 pound asparagus, steamed *al dente*, and kept hot. Let cool, cover and refrigerate for 2 days before serving. Serves 4 or as a garnish for any salad.

LAYERED LETTUCE SALAD

BETTY HARKER is an over-night celeb with her Layered Lettuce Salad. Layer in following order in 9x13 inch pyrex dish: 1/2 head or 2 C shredded head lettuce, 1 package thawed frozen peas, 1 C diced celery, 1/4 C chopped green pepper, 1/2 C chopped onion, 4 hard boiled eggs sliced, 8 slices or more crisp bacon broken into bits.

Spread like a frosting: 2 C mayonnaise mixed with 2 T sugar. Sprinkle the top with 1 C grated sharp cheese. You may make it ahead and even better yet the night before you wish to serve it.

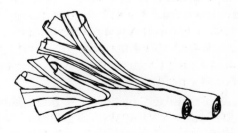

CRUNCHY PEA SALAD

A favorite from the HONOLULU ACADEMY OF ARTS GARDEN CAFE is Crunchy Pea Salad. Combine the following: 1 (10 ounce) package of frozen petite peas, thawed, 1 C chopped celery, 1/4 C chopped green onion (3 to 4 inches of green tops), 1 C chopped cashews or macadamia nuts and 1/4 C crisp bacon bits. Mix together 1 C sour cream, 1/4 C Garden Cafe dressing and 1/2 t salt and fold in gently. Serve well chilled on bed of crisp leaf lettuce.

PICKLED BEETS

A jar of Pickled Beets in the refrig is always great insurance. Use either canned whole or fresh. Quarter and put in wide mouth jar, drop in a sliced onion, 1 T plus of pickling spices, shake of garlic salt and enough oil and vinegar to your taste and to cover. Keeps quite a while and ready for any emergency.

TUNA AND CUCUMBER SALAD

FATIMA CAMERON'S Tuna and Cucumber Salad is a great solution to a summer luncheon served with *taro* muffins. Soften 1 envelope gelatin in 2 T lemon juice in large mixer bowl. Add 1/2 C boiling chicken broth and stir to dissolve. Add 1/2 C mayonnaise, 1/4 C milk, 2 T chopped parsley, 1 T minced green onion, 1 t each prepared mustard and dried dill weed, 1/4 t pepper.

Beat until well mixed, chill 30 minutes and beat again until frothy. Fold in 1 (7 ounce) can tuna and 1/2 C shredded cucumber. Pour into 2-cup mold to chill and firm. Serves 4.

Combine *peanut butter, honey, mayon-naise, and sesame seeds* to a salad dressing consistency and pour over fresh fruit salads.

Jazz up plain mayonnaise with chopped parsley, chives, Worcestershire sauce and a little hot mustard.

THOUSAND ISLAND DRESSING

Don't forget Thousand Island Dressing! Combine chopped hard boiled eggs, mayonnaise, ketsup, small amount of vinegar, salt and pepper and mix well. Kids are bound to eat their salad then.

Try adding some curry powder, powdered ginger and chopped mango chutney to taste to a basic chicken salad! Then watch the puzzled but delighted expressions of your guests!

FRUITED CHICKEN SALAD

MARILYN SULLIVAN'S Fruited Chicken Salad: Heat together one 3-ounce package cream cheese, softened, with 1/2 C real or imitation sour cream and add at least 2 t of salt. Add 1 C drained mandarin orange segments, 3/4 C diced celery, 1/2 C chopped walnuts, 1-1/2 C diced cooked chicken meat, 2 T mayonnaise and toss gently. Chill overnight.

Taste and add more salt if necessary. Very gently toss in most of a cup of chilled jellied cranberry sauce, cubed. Serve on beds of lettuce and garnish with remaining cranberry cubes. Serves 4.

ONO MACARONI SALAD

LYNN SMITH'S Ono Macaroni Salad: Combine 2 C cooked hot salad or elbow macaroni, one 16-ounce carton cottage cheese, one

10-ounce package frozen peas and carrots (thawed), and 1/2 C each chopped green pepper, green onions, and bottled Italian dressing. Mix well, cover and chill for 2 hours or more. Just before serving combine in smaller bowl: 1 8-ounce carton sour cream, 2 T lemon juice, 1/2 t powdered mustard, 1/4 t salt and pepper to taste. Stir to mix well and fold into macaroni mixture. 6-8 servings.

SEAFOOD MOUSSE

JOSEPHINE DINGHAM gives you a choice of this *Mousse. . . crabmeat, salmon, tuna or fish*.

Dissolve 2 envelopes gelatin in 1/4 C water.

In saucepan combine 1 large package cream cheese, 1 C mayonnaise, 1 can mushroom soup (undiluted), 1 small grated onion, 1/2 t salt, and 1 T Worcestershire sauce.

Heat over hot water until cheese melts and it is smooth. Keep stirring, add gelatin, and blend well. Add 1 C finely chopped celery and 1 C of your choice of seafood. Mix well and pour into wet mold and chill.

Unmold on cold platter and decorate with tomato wedges, sprigs of watercress, parsley and crispy lettuce.

CUCUMBER SALAD

ENA SROAT'S Cucumber Salad is perfect for fish dinners. Dissolve 2 packages lime jello in 1-1/2 C hot water.

Grind together: 1 C peanuts, 1 large cucumber, 1 small onion, and drain off any juice.

Mix 1 C mayonnaise with 1 C cottage cheese. Now put them all together and it makes 12 salad molds or 1 large mold.

JADE TREE SALAD DRESSING

CLAIRE GREGORCYK serves Jade Tree Salad Dressing over iceberg lettuce and sometimes adds canned mandarin oranges or fresh oranges and/or grapefruit sections.

Mix well: 1/4 C toasted sesame seeds or sunflower seeds: 1-1/2 C safflower oil, 2/3 C tarragon vinegar, 2 t salt, 1 t dry mustard, 1/2 t each garlic powder and pepper, 1/4 C grated parmesan cheese, and 1 can sliced water chestnut chopped. Keep refrigerated.

KAUAI CANOES

JINNY LIVERMORE, a frequent visitor to Hawaii, introduced islanders to Kauai Canoes. Parboil 1 zucchini per person, cool, cut in half lengthwise, remove pulp, core and seeds. Put in pyrex pan and fill shells with sliced onion and garlic. Cover with French dressing then aluminum foil and refrigerate overnight.

To prepare for serving, remove shells from marinade and discard all garlic and onion. Place 2 each on beds of crisp lettuce. Line shells (canoes) with mayonnaise then stack thinly sliced cherry tomatoes lengthwise to fill each canoe. Add a bit more salad dressing and sprinkle top generously with dry grated parmesan cheese.

Sandwiches

THE BROWN BAG FILLER - SANDWICHES

Discouraging, isn't it when you go to a lot of fuss and bother to make up fancy sandwiches for the family outing and the kiddies rebel with the old battle cry... "Where's the peanut butter and jelly!" Well, to each his own. A tasty sandwich and a hearty salad can be lunch fit for a queen any day.

Be sure the bread is fresh. A loaf of unsliced bread is a luxury today but thinly sliced bread makes the best sandwiches. . . so better we make our own!

Slather either mayonnaise or butter on two slices of bread, spread your filling evenly and smoothly to the edges, cover and then trim off the crusts. Cut in half or quarters but wrap the finished product stacked in twos securely in saran wrap or wax paper and cover with damp tea towel.

Set up a *Sandwich Bar* at your next luncheon or picnic! Prepare several cartons of different fillings. . . egg, tuna, corn beef, peanut butter and honey; bags of sliced onions and tomatoes; crisp dry lettuce leaves; individually wrapped slices of cheese squares; jars of peanut butter and jelly for the protestors and lots of mayonnaise and pickles!

Supply white and brown bread, crackers and home made banana bread for the sweet toothed. Let them concoct their own sandwiches.

TUNA SANDWICH

Tuna sandwiches always taste better if you add a squirt of lemon juice, some dill weed, chopped parsley, finely chopped celery or green onion, onion salt and ground pepper to the mixture.

JAN SCHULTE suggests slicing the canned Boston brown bread with raisins to any thickness and filling with a mixture of all kinds of chopped fresh veggies and mayonnaise.

EGG AND KAMABOKO

Egg and Kamaboko mixture will stymie your friends. Chop *kamaboko* fine and add half and half proportions of chopped eggs and add seasonings and mayonnaise for spreading consistency.

WATERCRESS-CREAM CHEESE

Watercress-Cream Cheese sandwiches are delicious with a cold soup or trimmed and quartered served for pupus. Blend finely chopped watercress with softened cream cheese, dash of tabasco and enough mayonnaise for spreading consistency. Spread between slitely mayonnaised thinly sliced bread.

Or Watercress-Bacon is good, too. Fry 10 slices bacon *crisp*, drain and crumble. Wash, dry and chop very fine handful of tender watercress stalks and combine with either cream cheese or plain mayonnaise and tabasco sauce for spreading consistency.

CORNED BEEF

Corned Beef sandwiches are hearty for picnics yet delectable as pupus, too. Combine a can of corned beef with 3 stalks whole green onions finely chopped, dash of ketsup, Worcestershire and enough mayonnaise for spreading consistency. Some like it with pickle relish, too, but it gets a bit runny. Take the mixture on picnics in plastic bowl and spread on hard tacks or between slices of bread.

For the pupu route. . . add 1/2 to 1 C grated sharp cheese to the mixture, spread between very good rye or brown bread slices. Toast both sides on 2nd oven rack under broiler. You may cut the quarters after toasting or before.

DEVILED EGG

When making Deviled Egg sandwiches, it is much easier and more uniform to grate the hard boiled egg rather than chopping with knife or fork. There are many additions once you've moistened with mayonnaise but creaming in some cream cheese gives it a special taste and texture treat.

HOT CRAB SANDWICH

Hot Crab Sandwich: Line a flat buttered baking dish with 4 slices of de-crusted buttered white bread, top generously with slices of sharp cheese, grated round onion or chopped green onions, your favorite seasoning, then sprinkle 1 can crab (or shrimp or chopped chicken) and cover with 4 more slices buttered bread. Pour a mixture of 1-1/2 C milk and 3 well beaten eggs over the sandwiches. Cover and refrigerate overnight. Bake covered in 450 oven 40 minutes and 20 minutes uncovered and serve immediately.

SPECIAL TUNA

PAM BECK'S Special Tuna Sandwich: Butter halved English muffins. Combine can of tuna, 2 chopped hard boiled eggs, mayonnaise, curry powder to taste and spread on muffins. Add layer of mango chutney and top with sliced squares of Jack and cheddar cheese to form checkerboard effect. Pop in oven to broil and warm through. Pam serves a fresh green salad with this and ice tea.

CHICKEN SANDWICH SPREAD

Chicken Sandwich Spread: Mix 2 C chopped chicken, 1/2 C finely chopped celery, 1/4 C finely chopped parsley or watercress, 1/2 clove minced garlic, and 4 T mayonnaise. Season with salt, pepper and paprika and blend well. Spread between buttered slices of white bread.

AVOCADO AND MACADAMIA NUT FILLING

Avocado and Macadamia Nut Filling: Mash flesh of 1 medium avocado, add 1/4 C crushed nuts, 1 T lemon juice, 1 T pickled small white onions, chopped, salt, pepper and paprika. Blend well and spread between thin slices of rye or whole wheat bread.

CREAM CHEESE, ALMOND AND MINT FILLING

Cream Cheese, Almond and Mint Filling: Beat together 1 small package cream cheese, 2 T chopped macadamia nuts and 1 t mint jelly. Spread between slices of whole wheat bread.

30. . . _____. . . SANDWICHES

Herbs

WITH FRESH HERBS

Someone once said that "Our Creator instructed us when He first placed us on this earth that this earth will be our mother. She is a mother to us, giving us all that is necessary for a continuing life. She gives us the food we eat this very day. She has been faithful to her instructions for many thousands of years!"

How true.

And summertime seems to accentuate this more than any other time of year. If we have vegetable gardens we are reaping a bountiful harvest of spring planting and can bypass the produce departments in the markets.

Island fruits are at their peak and we should take advantage of this time of year to use and preserve the abundant crops even though it means a lot of extra work. You can always pick and freeze and do the hard work later.

Remember the gracious old homes sitting midst sprawling lawns, formal gardens and tremendous vegetable gardens that supplied the family and all the live-in help and then some?

Mango, tamarind, avocado, breadfruit, coconut, and sour-sop trees grew to great proportions.

Grape arbors were tucked away. Always a little clump of sweet sugar cane, and the mulberry tree was the joy of the "caterpillar crowd."

Valley homes were sure to have a few mountain apple trees, guavas growing wild, and lychee trees. Figs on the sprawling tree were well protected from the birds with old mosquito nets. The fresh figs were served with luscious cream! Gnarled and lichened citrus trees abounded and bananas of all varieties. Then came the era of developers and today properties are smaller but the treasured fruit trees remain.

Even apartment dwellers can get in the act with potted citrus, baby tomatoes, well-pruned eggplant bush, and fabulous herbs. Actually the combined fragrance could create quite a garden-like atmosphere.

Why, there's no end to the possibilities in this department. . . think of brewing up your own herb teas, the exotic potpourris, sachets, and imaginative cooking. Goodness, you can become a master magician transforming common old dishes into tantalizing concoctions.

For starters in pots the basics might be basil, parsley, chives and mint. . . good old stand-bys. Then as the fever mounts, you'll be adding oregano, dill, lemon grass, rosemary, etc. etc. etc. etc.

As a matter of fact, why not potted Hawaiian medicinal plants as a unique venture? There seems to be an upsurge in natural herbs for medicinal value today. But back to basics. Usually if you get to the plant sales of churches or schools early enough you can scoop up the herb seedlings. They seem to go first.

One word of warning in cooking: don't get carried away and go "herb-happy." Start slowly until your experimenting with small quantities is for sure. Remember, too, that dried herbs are three times as strong as fresh ones!

CHIVES

Someone once referred to Chives as the most ladylike member of the onion family. . . I like that! Chives for cream cheese, cucumbers, topping for soups, omelets, and tossed green salads.

PARSLEY

Parsley is best for garnishing, deep-fried tempura style, or chopped for a hundred different dishes. Jazz up plain mayonnaise with chopped parsley, chives, Worcestershire sauce and a little mustard.

MINT

Mint is a must for iced-tea and various fruit punches and that famous southern julep.

Mint sauce for lamb: Simmer 1/4 C vinegar, less than half a C of water, 1 T dried mint leaves for about 5 minutes. Strain. Add 1/4 C water, 1 T lemon juice, 2 T sugar, 1/4 t salt and 2 T dried mint leaves. Bring to boil and simmer for few minutes. Chill before serving.

CELERY LEAF TOPS

Don't throw away those beautiful Celery Leaf Tops! Pat dry and place them on a cookie sheet and leave them in warm oven to dry out until crispy, then bottle and use for flavoring.

CELERY SEED

Celery Seed is a must for a worthwhile potato salad and cole slaw, pickles and some chutney. Cole Slaw: Combine 3 T heated wine vinegar, and 1 T celery seed and add to 1/2 C mayonnaise. Stir in T or more of fresh chopped parsley and pour over 1 medium size cabbage shredded as fine as you can. Toss and season with salt and pepper to taste. Chill well.

SESAME SEEDS

Sesame Seeds in breads, pastries, salad and to flavor veggies. Try sprinkling some on toppings for casseroles. It gets more and more popular.

ROSEMARY

Rosemary is the meat herb, and a threesome for lamb is garlic, rosemary and mint.

BAY LEAVES

Bay Leaves for stews, soup stocks, pickles, and seafood. . . but remember to remove before serving.

PAPRIKA

Keep Paprika bottle in fridge. Used mostly for garnish as it tends to get lost amongst other strong herbs.

BASIL

Basil is a tomato's best friend!

BOUQUET GARNI

Bouquet Garni. . . Bay leaves, thyme, parsley, and basil tied in cheesecloth, removed before serving.

FINES HERBES

Fines Herbes. . . Herbs chopped fine to be added directly to a dish. . . stew or omelet. . . parsley, basil and chives. . . parsley, chervil and chives.

FRESH HERBS WITH FISH

"Fresh herbs give fish a better aroma and flavor but you have to use twice as much as dry which is stronger. Before adding to anything, crumble the dry herbs to release the odor", said VERNA LAZRNICK at a session of the "CLE-VER GOURMET COOKING SCHOOL".

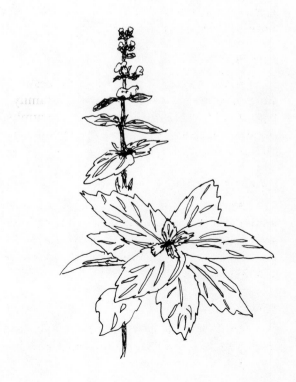

Vegetables...

OUR EARTHLY BLESSINGS
VEGGIES

Lucky the lady who has a vegetable garden at her disposal! The infinite difference in fresh picked produce versus store-bought or frozen is more than worth the weeding and tilling!

Ears of corn from stalk to pot! Tomatoes eaten still warm from the vine and baby carrots to nibble. You'll never rue the day you start with a few packets of essential seeds and watch your garden grow.

Lettuce is known mostly for its merits in salad. However, Indians were using lettuce leaves to preserve the moisture in cooking foods long before the white man arrived. . . not unlike the Hawaiians who wrapped their foods in *ti* leaves to cook and store.

Soy beans is one of the easiest and most prolific crops to grow and books of recipes from this vegetable have been written. It is chock full of protein and can be used in hundreds of ways.

Keep the cover on underground veggies.

Leave above grown veggies uncovered.

Keep parsley fresh in a clean jar in the refrig.

Happy digging!

OVEN BAKED CORN

If you don't believe the 'Indian bit' here's a point of proof. JAN SCHULTEN, a frequent island visitor wrote from Maine: "Am sending this recipe which I thought might interest you for you here in Hawaii have such dandy corn. Smear shucked corn with butter, majoram and rosemary, blended. Wrap each ear in Romaine lettuce and place in flat pan, and seal with foil. Pop into 400 oven for 25-30 minutes. It breaks all the rules but it's divine. You have to try to believe."

LIMA BEAN CASSEROLE

PHOEBE PUMMEL'S Lima Bean Casserole is almost a meal in itself it's so good. Combine and mix well 2 or 3 cans (8-ounce) lima beans, chopped onion, 1 can condensed tomato soup, 3/4 C brown sugar, 1 t mustard and dash of ketchup. Pour into casserole, lay strips of bacon on top or combine sliced Portuguese sausage with beans and bake in 350 oven for 2-3 hours. Great Pot-Luck Supper dish.

BARBARA TILLEY'S family cook, LIZA dictated this recipe to her 20 years ago with strict instructions. . . 'no short cuts', but Barbara always uses frozen spinach.

GARDEN TORTE

LIZA'S Garden Torte: Steam 3 pounds spinach in 1 C boiling water 5 minutes and finely chop. Slice 4 medium zucchini unpeeled in 1/4 inch circles. Saute in oil with cover on pan to slightly steam. *Do not cook thoroughly.* Add 3 T grated parmesan to spinach. Add 4 eggs one at a time, whip thoroughly between each addition. Soak 2 slices of bread in 1/4 C sweet cream and whip into mixture and add salt to taste and 1/4 C chopped parsley.

Now fold in zucchini and 3 sliced green onions. Be careful not to break the slices of squash. Turn into buttered 8x2x12 inch baking dish and bake in 350 oven for about 45 minutes. Test with straw as you would with a cake. 12 servings.

SWEET POTATO

Sweet Potato is a good change. Boil 4 yams until tender, peel and mash. Add sufficient butter and 2 T brown sugar and a can of thawed frozen coconut milk. Beat until light and fluffy, turn into buttered casserole dish, dot with butter and bake 350 oven for 30 minutes.

ONION CHEESE PIE

Onion Cheese Pie is a change from creamed onions at holiday time. *Crust:* Combine 1 cube melted butter or oleo and add 1-1/2 C soda cracker crumbs. Press crumb mixture into a buttered 10-inch pie pan.

Filling: Brown 2-1/2 C thinly sliced onions in 2 T butter or oleo and spread on crust. Scald 1-1/4 C milk, remove from heat. Beat 3 eggs slightly and add hot milk stirring constantly until well blended. Season with salt and pepper and add 2 C grated cheddar cheese and mix thoroughly. Pour mixture over onions. Bake in 350 oven for 40 minutes or until inserted knife comes out clean. Serve at once. 6-8 servings.

TARO

Taro is a basic Hawaiian vegetable, but unfortunately seldom used at dinner tables except in the form of *poi.* Peel and boil the *taro* until very tender, like potato by testing with fork. Change water twice while boiling.

TARO CAKES

Taro Cakes: Drain and mash enough for 2 C while hot adding a little water and generous dollops of butter to melt. Mix well and sift over 1 t sugar, 1/2 t salt, 2 t baking powder. Form into small flat cakes with wet hands, make hole in middle and fill with butter. Bake 350 oven 20-30 minutes until nicely browned.

TARO CAKES

ANNIE SHAW FARDEN'S Taro Cakes. Peel and quarter fresh *taro* and boil until fork-done, changing the water several times. Mash down well and gradually add only enough water to make it the consistency of biscuit dough.

Knead 2 C *taro* and mix in 4 t baking powder, 1/4 t salt and dash of sugar. Roll on floured board to 1-1/2 inches. Cut with smallest biscuit cutter. Drop in heated deep fat (like donuts) until crispy and brown. Drain on brown paper and serve hot. They should be crispy outside and gooey inside when you pop them open to add more butter!

TARO PUFFS

Here's another verson from the *taro* pamphlet the ladies of the PACIFIC TROPICAL BOTANICAL GARDEN edited. Baked or fried Taro Puffs: Combine 2 t baking powder, 1 t salt, 1/2 C flour, 2 C mashed cooked *taro*. Mix well, shape into balls and place in buttered muffin tin. Make indentation on the top and place a piece of butter in it. Bake 475 oven 10 to 15 minutes. Patties can be deep fried until golden brown.

STEAMED BREADFRUIT

And here is their Steamed Breadfruit from the Breadfruit Pamphlet. Breadfruit at any state of ripeness may be steamed in a covered steamer for an hour or more, until tender. Steam it whole and unpeeled, or peeled and quartered. Serve immediately with butter and salt and pepper. . . and you'll want *lots* of butter.

SPINACH AND CHEESE QUICHE

From the files of the CLE-VER GOURMET COOKING SCHOOL comes this superb and easy Spinach and Cheese Quiche. Saute 2 T minced shallots or green onions briefly in 3 T butter. Drain well, add 1-1/4 C chopped blanched spinach and 1 C chopped blanched watercress. Stir over moderate heat to evaporate any excess water. Stir in 1/2 t salt, 1/8 t each pepper, nutmeg, dill and taste for seasoning. Add 1/4 C each grated romano and feta cheese. Gradually stir in 4 lightly beaten eggs mixed with 2 C milk. Pour into prepared pastry shell, sprinkle with grated Swiss cheese or romano, dot with butter and bake 25-30 minutes in 375 oven. Don't forget to give it 10 minutes to pull itself together!

TARO CAKES

CAROL WILCOX cooks her Taro Cakes differently and with a new innovation! Boil up 3 scrubbed large *taro* corms in water to cover, bring to boil, change water and continue boiling until you're sure they're done. . . test by spearing easily with fork. Cool to touch, peel and *grate on big puka of cheese grater.* Add 1-2 cubes melted butter, salt and pepper. Form into patties. . . bake, fry or freeze!

ZUCCHINI CASSEROLE

MIDGE HERBERT'S Zucchini Casserole: In mixing bowl beat 4 eggs, add 1/4 C flour, 1/4 C grated parmesan cheese, 1-1/4 t salt, 3 T chopped parsley and thinly sliced green onion, minced clove of garlic, 3/4 t oregano, 1/4 t pepper, and stir in 1-1/4 pound finely chopped zucchini. Turn into 1-1/2 quart baking dish, top with sliced peeled tomato, sprinkle with 1/4 C or more parmesan and bake uncovered 350 oven for 30 minutes or until custard sets.

BAKED BEANS

LEE BOYNTON'S Baked Beans go well with hamburgers on a picnic! Fry up some diced bacon, add 1 small onion to brown, combine in bean pot with 2 1-pound 12-ounce cans pork and beans, 1/2 C brown sugar, 2/3 C ketchup, 1 t dry mustard and 1/4 t ajinomoto, top with strips of bacon and bake 2 hours uncovered in 350 oven.

EASY SPINACH SOUFLEE

Easy Spinach Souflee: Thoroughly drain 2 boxes frozen chopped spinach. Combine and mix thoroughly with 1 can cream of mushroom soup, 2 T dried onion soup mix, 3/4 C mayonnaise, 2 well beaten eggs, salt and pepper and 1/4 C grated parmesan cheese. Sprinkle top with bacon bits and more parmesan. Pop in 350 oven for 30 mintues or when knife comes out clean.

MONGO BEANS

Mongo Beans are good to sprout. . . try it. So cruncy, delicious and healthful. You can find them in the Oriental department in cellophane packages. In a clean mayonnaise jar, add sterilized water and cool, then add 2 T washed mongo beans and soak overnight. Drain, but wait. . . save the juice for soup or drink it as it's chock full of vitamins. Rinse the beans, drain, return to jar and cover with cheese cloth and leave in dark place. . . but not so dark you forget them! Repeat process for about 3 days and leave on the counter or window sill 4th day for greening purposes. Put in bowl of water to remove husks, drain well and refrigerate to keep crisp.

So good in salads or namasu, too. Mix them with some chopped ham, green onions sliced fine, salt and pepper and eggs. Drop by spoonfuls and fry like pancakes on hot griddle. Serve with soy and hot mustard sauce!

MONGO-BEAN FRENCH BEAN CASSEROLE

Mongo-bean French Bean Casserole: Thaw and drain French style string beans and combine with chopped water chestnuts or the Japanese mountain yam or Jerusalem artichokes, can of cream of mushroom soup, lots of parmesan and top with croutons, canned onion rings and more cheese. Just heat it through until bubbly so it will be still crunchy.

HOT CURRIED FRUITS

Hot Curried Fruits: Drain 1 pound can each pear slices, apricot halves, pineapple chunks, and halve maraschino cherries from 1 4-ounce jar. You may also add slices of your own papaya and bananas, too. Put into 1-1/2 quart casserole. Blend together 2 T soft butter, 2 T dark brown sugar, 1 or 2 t curry, 2 t cornstarch and 1/2 t lemon peel and sprinkle over fruit. Let stand for several hours to draw out juices and flavors and bake uncovered in 325 oven for 1/2 hour, turning several times.

HOT SLAW

SARAH WILDER'S Hot Slaw was a family favorite with baked ham.

Melt 4 T butter in saucepan, add 3 T flour, stir in 1-1/2 C milk and cook til thick then add 1 beaten egg.

Boil 1/2 C each vinegar and sugar then

add to flour mixture. Chop up 6 C raw cabbage and dry completely. Pour hot dressing over cabbage and serve immediately.

EGGPLANT CASSEROLE

NANCY VERA CRUZ'S Eggplant Casserole is tasty and can be done in advance. Wash, peel and slice 2 eggplants 1/4 inch thick, dip in beaten egg and then coat thoroughly with the seasoned flour. Fry in oil until brown.

In another pan combine and heat 2 small 8-ounce cans tomato sauce, 1/3 package spaghetti sauce mix. Layer the fried eggplant in casserole, top with heaping T of the tomato mixture and sprinkle grated white cheese and garlic powder over and continue layering. Pour any leftover egg from dipping over and bake 350 for 30 minutes covered.

BAKED PAPAYA

Baked Papaya is a great complement to curry especially, or lamb. Cut papaya in half and de-seed. Fill with T or more butter, dash of cinnamon, nutmeg and few squirts of lemon. Bake in 350 oven until easily pierced with fork but not mushy.

BANANA CASSEROLE

Try combining guava jelly and bananas to serve with a curry dinner. It's a good 'do-ahead' and there are variations to this, too. Allow 1 banana per person, actually most types are okay as long as you scrape the fine threads off well.

FRIED BANANAS

Fry Bananas in sufficient oleo over moderate heat to gently cook and brown. Add some lemon juice and a dash of cayenne pepper.

When bananas are cooked and nicely browned and still hot, dribble and stir in the guava jelly and pour into casserole to warm later. (Good way to use up jelly that didn't jell!).

FRIED RICE

Fried Rice is the best way to use up leftover rice and everyone loves it! In a large pan fry up some sliced bacon and when done add some oleo and brown sliced white onions, carrots, string beans and mushrooms. Add the cold rice, break it up and mix all together. Add soy to taste, crack an egg or two over and stir quickly. Cover and let steam over low fire. Before serving add chopped green onions, whites and tops, and either slivers of ham or roast pork.

ZUCCHINI PANCAKES

You like pancakes? Try these Zucchini Pancakes. . . In the blender combine a C of zucchini, 1/4-1/2 C onion chopped, 1/4 C green bell peppers, garlic salt and fine herbs,

2 eggs, 1/2 C milk and turn to chop. Then drizzle ready-mix biscuit mix until consistency of the kind of pancake batter you like. . . 'tick or tin'. Fry in a pan generously doused with oil. Make dollar size pancakes, freeze and use later for pupus. Or fry a large crepe size pancake and roll up left-over curry. Or serve plain with hot dogs or hash. . . don't waste a steak with these!

SOY BEANS

Soy Beans are easy to grow and a great addition to soups, stews or a sub for lima beans in making succotash. For *pupus* par boil them in pot with sprinkle of Hawaiian salt and leave in bowl with extra salt for guests to shell and enjoy.

ARTICHOKES

When cooking Artichokes, cover with water and add: bay leaf, slices of onion, sprigs of parsley, slices of lemon, chopped clove of garlic, dash of salad oil, salt and peppercorns, or even a T of pickling spices.

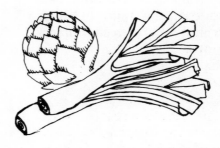

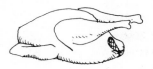

....Poultry....

OUR FINE FEATHERED FRIENDS
FOWL

Chix, turks and Cornish game hens are usually good buys when on sale. Grab as many as the traffic will bear in the ole freezer. . . worth it. You can 'dress' them in many styles. . . Hawaiian, Chinese, Japanese, elegant French, fancy or plain. They are a universal favorite with young and old. . . hot or cold.

If at all possible a chilled turkey for the holidays is so worth the difference in price. It's juicier, tenderer and doesn't come laced with all that unwanted butter under the guise of being self-basting!

Fresh chicken likewise.

Remember if you remove the stuffing after the first serving there's less chance of spoilage and you can re-heat it and the gravy for a second go-round. Some people bake stuffing separately in a casserole.

For some reason a sprinkling of lemon juice over the chicken makes it whiter and sweeter. When frying chicken, use tongs to turn as forks pierce and let out good juices!

Brown, turn once, turn twice, remove from pan and sop up excess grease on paper towels. The less you turn the less greasy the pieces.

And bless those carcasses. . . the soup pot welcomes any and all discards!

So you see, my friends, these birds go a long way!

MAYONNAISE CHICKEN

ALEX KAAUA'S Mayonnaise chicken is a super do-ahead. Prepare it all in the morning and just bring out to bake for dinner.

In a bowl put 1 C mayonnaise and dump in 2 pounds chicken thighs and 'lomi' until chicken is evenly coated. Make a mixture of 1 C bread crumbs, garlic powder, salt and pepper, parmesan cheese, and paprika and roll the pieces in this to coat evenly. Place pieces in foil-lined pan and bake in 350 oven for 45 minutes uncovered.

CHICKEN LUAU

A must at any *poi* supper. . . Chicken Luau: You may steam a whole chicken or chicken thighs, but steam it gently in or over water with sliced onions, chicken bouillon cubes and Hawaiian salt. When well done, cool, de-bone and remove all skin and any gristle, break into small pieces and return to stock. If you can't get the fresh luau leaves, don't fret. Cook up several boxes of frozen chopped spinach in salted water and drain every ounce of water out. . . you'll be amazed how little spinach is left, really. Combine this with the prepared chicken. . . about 1 C stock to 2 cups each chicken and spinach. You may freeze this. To serve bring to boil and keep hot. Add can of thawed frozen coconut milk but don't let it boil. . . the coconut milk is what makes this dish rich so add according to taste and you might want more salt, too.

To keep coconut milk from souring, combine 1 t salt with 1/2 C milk, bring to boil, let settle then add to pint frozen coconut milk.

BONELESS CHICKEN

JANE IBARA'S Boneless Chicken is scrumptious. Thaw 1 (2 lb. box) chicken thighs and de-bone, doesn't matter if it is in pieces. Combine and thoroughly mix: 4 T mochiko flour (in Oriental food section), 4 T sugar, 1/2 t salt, 5 T soy, 1/2 t ajinomoto, 2 T chopped green onions, 2 slightly beaten eggs, 1 small clove garlic minced and small piece of ginger chopped fine (optional).

Marinate chicken in this for at least 2 hours or longer turning to coat and fry in hot oil to brown. Garnish with parsley to serve. Lots of rice!

POULARDE DE BRUZELLES

CLAIRE BOOTH LUCE serves this chicken at special dinner parties. Poularde de Bruzelles: Rub the inside and out of 1 medium roasting chicken with salt and pepper. Split shells of 1 pound chestnuts crosswise and spread on baking sheet to roast in 425 oven until shells pop open. Remove shells and inner skins. Cook chestnuts in broth to cover, until soft; then puree them coarsely. Add 1 chopped chicken liver, 2 T butter, 2 eggs beaten, 2 T cream, 2 truffles chopped (optional), 1 T lemon juice, 2 T minced parsley, and nutmeg and sage to taste.

Fill chicken with stuffing, close with skewer and twine. Put chicken in heavy casserole and brush with 4 T melted butter. Brown well on all sides. Add 1 C red wine and enough hot water just to cover the bottom of the casserole. Cover tightly and cook for 1-1/2 hours, basting from time to time. Remove chicken to heated platter, scrape bottom of pot and add about 1/2 C water. Blend in 1 C sour cream and season to taste. Thicken sauce with a little cornstarch mixed with cold water. When thickened spoon sauce over baked chicken to give a glaze. Serve whole or in serving pieces with dressing removed.

SUPREME DE VOLAILLE A BLANC

From the CLE-VER GOURMET COOKING SCHOOL comes Supreme de Volaille a

Blanc. . . translated: boned chicken breast. Cleo Evans explained that the delicacy of this dish is not to overcook the chicken. Watch it. When it completely loses its pink, that is *the* moment to remove the pieces to platter! Rub 4 de-boned chicken breasts with 1/2 t lemon juice and sprinkle lightly with 1/4 t salt and pinch of white pepper. Heat 4 T butter in casserole until it is foaming. . . off heat quickly, roll the breasts in butter, lay a round of wax paper over them, cover the casserole and place in hot oven.

After 6 minutes, press the top of the supreme with your finger. If still soft, return to the oven for a moment or two. When the meat is springy to the touch the meat is done. Remove to warm platter and make *sauce:* Pour 1/4 C stock of chicken broth and 1/4 C dry white wine, Port, Madeira or Vermouth into the casserole with the cooking butter and boil down quickly over high heat until liquid is syrupy. Stir in 1 C whipping cream or half and half and boil down again over high heat until the cream has thickened slightly. Off heat. Taste carefully for seasoning, add drops lemon juice to taste. Pour sauce over the supremes, sprinkle with chopped parsley and serve.

ITALIAN STYLE CHICKEN

Italian Style Chicken: Cut 2-3 pound chicken into suitable pieces and brown well in olive oil in Dutch oven or heavy skillet. When well browned add 2 T parsley chopped fine, 2 cloves garlic chopped fine, pinch of rosemary, salt and pepper and about 1 C white wine. Cover and cook very slowly until chicken is tender, basting and turning frequently so each piece is well flavored. Add minced onion if you like. Good with either noodles or rice.

GOURMET CHICKEN

DEBBIE PRATT'S Gourmet Chicken: Thinly coat chicken breasts with *Pickappeppa* (akin to Worcestershire Sauce) and either bake at 350 for an hour or broil over charcoal. Use the sauce sparingly, though. . . piquant and a little goes a long way but delicious.

COQ AU VIN

MARGARET COMMUNIEUX'S Coq Au Vin for 4. Brown 12 pieces of chicken thighs in 1-1/2 ounce butter then add 10 small onions, 1/2 clove chopped garlic, 1 bouquet garni (parsley and bay leaf) salt and pepper and 2 ounces mushrooms. Then add 1 C brandy and flambe (put a fire to it). When the fire is out, add 3 C burgundy. Cook on medium heat for about 30 minutes.

CHICKEN OPTIONS

Chicken Options: In a brown bag combine 1 t salt, 1/2 t celery salt, 1/4 t garlic salt, 1/4 t nutmeg and sufficient flour to shake and coat 2 pounds chicken. . . thighs or whatever. If you don't want the bag to burst on you, try slipping it into a protective cellophane vegetable bag. Shake well to coat nicely and leave bag on counter for a while to set coating. Then brown in 4 T butter or oleo or both or liquid oil like the TV ads and place in shallow baking dish.

And here are the options. . . Style 1. . . Combine syrup from one no. 2 can pineapple slices (1 cup), 1/2 C soy, 2 T brown sugar and pour over chicken. Cover and bake 350 oven for 1 hour. Serve with sauteed pieces of the sliced pineapple.

Option 2. . . Combine and pour over 1 part burgundy, 1 part sugar, 1 part soy and bake covered for 1 hour.

Tantalizing option 3. . . spice your browned chicken with the syrup and pieces of candied ginger or orange marmalade and steam (covered) to cook through and melt the accents.

BUTTERMILK CHICKEN

Buttermilk Chicken: Dip pieces of chicken in buttermilk and then in mixture of Bisquick, dry mustard and paprika plus seasoning. Brown evenly in sizzling oil. Remember the tongs! Place on paper towels to absorb excess grease and keep warm in oven.

CHICKEN CASSEROLE

Chicken Casserole is excellent for a girlie luncheon. Grease a 12x8x2 casserole dish. Cube 4 slices of bread and spread on the bottom of dish, put 3 C cooked chicken cut up on the cubes, cover with 6 slices of decrusted white bread. Mix 2 T grated onion, 1 C celery cut fine and 1/2 C mayonnaise and spread on top of bread. Beat 4 eggs and mix with 1 C evaporated milk and 1-1/2 C chicken broth. Pour over all. Cover and place in refrigerator overnight. Then bake 20 minutes in 350 oven, remove from oven and pour over the top 1 can of mushroom soup, undiluted. Sprinkle with cheese and paprika. Bake an additional 30 minutes and serve immediately.

TURKEY EN PANCAKE

Turkey En Pancake: Make pancake batter with the boxed cornbread mix and reserve. Make your own rich cream sauce, add some sherry, about 3 or 4 T. Reserve half and to the other half add: either diced turkey or chicken, sliced mushrooms, chopped parsley, minced onion and your own seasoning. Now fry up the pancakes, place turkey mixture on top, roll them up, place in buttered casserole, cover with the plain cream sauce, sprinkle parmesan cheese and bake till bubbling and brown.

Here's some changes for the stuffing routine.

Try adding golden raisins or slices of cored and peeled apples.

RICE STUFFING

DOTTIE KANEAIAKALA'S Rice Stuffing: For 15 lb turkey. Cook 3 C rice, cool slightly, fluffing with fork. Saute 2 medium onions, chopped, 1-1/2 C chopped celery in 3 T butter till soft (do not brown). Add chopped cooked giblets and cook gently one minute more, add 3/4 t thyme flakes, 1 T parsley flakes, 3/4 t poultry seasoning. Combine with rice mixing well. If desired add 1 can chopped mushrooms. Stuff your bird!

GIBLET STUFFING

A super elegant stuffing is from the files of PETER ARIOLI for a 20 lb. turkey or less quantities for chicken, pheasant or other fowls according to the judgement of the "Cook"!

Stuffing: Use the giblets and livers of fowl plus extra 1 pound each. In fry pan put 2 T oil, heat slightly and add 3-4 cloves garlic chopped; brown lightly to extract flavor. Add chopped giblets, stir, add 1 C claret wine, 3 dry bay leaves, salt and pepper, cook and stir til giblets are cooked. Put all in bowl but remove bay leaves. Repeat process with livers. In big mixing bowl scoop out center of large loaf stale white bread (no crusts). Put 1-1/2 C shelled walnuts through grinder or blender and add to bread. Grind liver and giblets and add to bowl. Mix well with juices from fry pan and 1 C chicken stock. Add 1 C milk, a little at a time til mixture is well blended and consistency of sausage meat or hamburger, then 1 t powdered sage, salt and pepper to taste. Mix well and test flavors.

Slather chunks of butter and salt and pepper inside dried cavity of bird and stuff loosely and sew up with fine string on needle. Cook bird 20 minutes per pound and baste frequently. Stuffing will taste like a heavenly 'pate de foie gras' and delicious hot or cold!

MARINATED CHICKEN

BEE FRELINGHUYSEN'S Marinated Chicken is great party fare served with fluffy white rice and steamed fresh baby carrots. Cut up 2 fresh fryers and marinate overnight in 2 6-ounce cans orange juice concentrate, 3 cloves minced garlic, and 4 T finely chopped parsley. Turn frequently.

Next day combine 1/2 C each golden raisins and sherry. Set aside.

Heat 1/4 C olive oil and 3 T oleo in large frying pan. Season 3/4 C flour with 3 t each salt and paprika and coat each piece of chicken. Brown lightly. Remove pieces from pan.

Melt 3 T oleo in skillet, add orange juice marinade, 1/2 C sherry, cook and stir until glazed. Add the chicken and spoon sauce to cover. Top with 1/2 C slivered almonds or macadamia nuts and the raisins and sherry mix. Simmer 45 minutes.

SAVORY STUFFING

Savory Stuffing a la CHRIS PALAY-CAY. . . for a 20 lb. turkey. Cube 1 pullman loaf stale white bread in a large bowl. Fry bacon slices until crisp, add chopped celery, onion, parsley, salt and pepper, sage, thyme and poultry seasoning to taste. Add to the bread, moisten with soup stock, crack in a few eggs (like other good cooks Chris uses leftovers and suggests adding any corn bread or sausage meat you might have), mix thoroughly, place in greased pan, dot with butter, cover with wax paper, bake 1-1/2 hours in 350 oven. Do ahead, refrigerate. Reheat to serve.

PUPULE CHICKEN

ENA SROAT'S *Pupule* Chicken is a winner. Combine 1 C mayonnaise with 1 T parmesan cheese, 1/2 t each dry mustard, sage, and soy. Coat 8 to 10 thighs with this and place in shallow baking dish. Give them a light dusting of garlic salt and pepper. Cover with 2 C grated sour dough bread.

Drizzle with 4 or 5 T melted butter then a very light dusting of Salad Supreme seasoning. Cover loosely with foil and bake in 400 oven for 1 hour or until tender. 4 to 5 servings.

ZESTY CORN STUFFING BALLS

These Zesty Corn Stuffing Balls are excellent with chicken or pork. In saucepan cook 1/2 C each chopped onion and celery in 4 T butter until tender. Add 1 17-ounce can cream style corn, 1/2 C water, 1 T poultry seasoning, 1/4 t pepper and bring to boil.

Pour over 1 8-ounce package herb-seasoned stuffing mix, toss lightly and stir in 3 slightly beaten eggs. Shape into 8 balls. Place in 9x9x2 inch baking pan, pour 1/2 C melted butter over and bake in 375 oven for about 30 minutes. You may refrigerate them until ready to bake.

CORNISH GAME HENS

Cornish Game Hen: Thaw birds in refrigerator, rinse with salt water and pat dry. Chop liver and gizzard and fry in butter with chopped onion, bits of mushroom and chopped parsley. . . amount depends on number of birds.

Add either bread cubes or cook contents of box of mixed wild and regular rice according to directions and add to giblets. Season with sage and poultry seasoning and salt and pepper to taste.

Stuff birds loosely and skewer opening. Slather with butter and bake until brown and crisp. . . about an hour to an hour and a half.

If Cornish game hens are larger than 1 pound, split them in half, sprinkle with salt and pepper, slather with butter, and cook cut side down in roaster with just a bit of water. Bake in 375 oven about 45 minutes or until done.

WALNUT STUFFING

This Walnut Stuffing should stuff 6 1-pound Cornish hens. Put 3 T bacon drippings in fry pan and saute 1 C each chopped onion and green pepper until tender. Add 6 cooked bacon slices crumbled, 3 C cubed day-old bread,

1 C coarsely chopped walnuts, 1-1/2 t salt, 1/2 t each thyme and sage. Toss mixture lightly to mix thoroughly and stuff hens loosely. Roast breast side up 1 hour in 350-400 degree oven.

Brush with *Basting Sauce*: Melt 1/2 C butter in small pot, remove from heat and add 1/2 C white wine, 1/2 t sage, 1-1/2 t salt and 1 clove garlic crushed, and baste occasionally while cooking.

ALA STUFFING

Ala Stuffing made from cracked wheat bulgar is a complete change and so easy to prepare. Melt 1/2 C butter or margarine in large skillet and add 1 C chopped celery, 1 medium onion, chopped, and 2 C uncooked *Ala*. Stir constantly until vegetables are tender and *Ala* is golden. Add 2 t salt, 1/4 t pepper, 1/2 t each sage and marjoram, 1 C chicken bouillon and 4 C cold water. Cover and bring to boil, reduce heat and simmer 15 minutes. Stuff poultry just before roasting. This makes 6 C of stuffing.

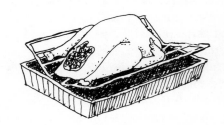

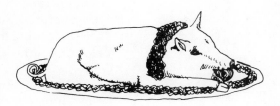

....Meats....

FROM THE PASTURE. . .
MEAT

Don't let the meat prices drive you to despair. Use your imagination. . . have some fun. . . experiment. . . use a little meat with lots of vegetables. Actually you really don't have to serve meat every night.

Cheaper cuts of meat can be fit for a king when you follow the slow-roasting method. Don't waste your money buying a roast under three pounds as it will shrink and dry out. The larger roasts are more economical, left-overs can be used in casseroles and slices of cold meat make hearty sandwiches.

If you're not sure of your oven, play it safe with a meat thermometer.

LAMB SHANKS

Lamb Shanks are a tasty change and a good buy when they're on special, so stock up on them. Remove the gristle and outer membrane from the shanks and shake well in a bag of seasoned flour. . . salt, thyme, rosemary, oregano and pepper. Drop several buds of garlic in a pan of hot oil and add the floured shanks. . . but remember to remove the buds when burned.

This takes a bit of standing over the hot pan but do brown them nicely and evenly and if possible to a crisp. Drain off all the grease, return shanks to pan and add water to scrape off the 'leavings' and then either leave in pan or place in casserole (crockpot is perfect for this one). Add quartered onions, several slices of lemon, dash of nutmeg, bay leaf and extra shakes of thyme, rosemary and oregano, chopped parsley and either lots of red wine or canned beef broth so it can simmer gently for hours until the meat begins to fall from the bones. It does have a tendency to be greasy so be sure and serve it piping hot and eat immediately.

Better yet, cook it the day before, pour gravy into bowl, wrap shanks in foil and refrigerate. Next day lift off lard and combine again in casserole and heat to serve. Also, a little sour cream added to gravy perks it up. Baked potatoes and baked whole tomatoes are excellent with this.

LAMB RIBS OR NECKS

When and if you see lean, meaty Lamb Ribs or Necks in the market, grab them. They stew up beautifully, and the meat is tender and sweet. . . not to mention the thrifty buy. You might have to buy about 4 to 5 pounds because it does boil down and there is quite a bit of fat. Toss it in a pot (crockpot?) and bring it to a good rolling boil for a few minutes then dump out that scummy water, refill to cover meat, add slivers of garlic, sliced onions, thyme, bay and rosemary leaves and salt and pepper to taste. Simmer this slowly for at least 2 hours or until the meat is tender and begins to fall from the bones. Wrap the meat in aluminum foil and pour the liquid into a bowl or wide-mouth jar and refrigerate. The next day lift off the crust of fat from the liquid and cut off some of the fat from the meaty pieces and combine the two and return to pot. Now take your choice. . . add curry powder and thicken; or add gingersnap crumbs, some ground ginger, thicken and serve.

EASY BAKED BEEF STEW

Easy Baked Beef Stew: On ample heavy duty foil or in casserole place 2 pounds lean beef stew, sprinkle with a package of dehydrated onion soup mix, add 1 C sherry, Worcestershire sauce, carton of sour cream and bake at 200 for 2 hours. Serve this one over buttered egg noodles with a green tossed salad.

CHOP SUEY

Chop Suey for dinner may mean spending the day leisurely chopping up all the veggies so they look professional (cut on a slant). Bag them individually and put in refrigerator until cooking time. Soak 3 pounds sliced beef a half hour before frying in marinade of soy, *sake* or bourbon, shredded finger of ginger, crushed clove of garlic, dash of sugar and salt and pepper.

Fry meat in hot fat quickly and set aside. Now bring out the packages of the veggies. Add in the following order to the slightly oiled pan. . . onions, carrots, green peppers, white turnips, cauliflower rosettes, celery, string beans, dried mushrooms, Chinese peas, package of bean sprouts, add the meat and keep stirring so vegetables don't get overcooked.

Add sauce from meat, sprinkle 2 t sugar, 1/2 C soy, 1/2 or more C water, leeetle bit more liquor, bring to a boil to thicken with paste of 2 T cornstarch and a little water. Add chopped watercress and green onions on top, test seasoning of gravy and correct. Cover pan while bubbling and turn off. Serve immediately before the veggies go limp, and have *lots of rice.*

MEAT LOAF

A good Meat Loaf is easy on the budget and good cold in sandwiches the next day. Combine 1-1/2 pound good ground round, 1-1/2 C bread crumbs, 2/3 C diced cheese, 1/2 C chopped onion, round or green or both, 2 T chopped green pepper, 2 t salt, 1 small bay leaf, thyme, garlic salt, 2 beaten eggs, 10-ounce can tomato puree. Mix thoroughly and shape into loaf and cook in moderate oven for 45 minutes to an hour.

MEAT LOAF

JEAN ANN MILNOR'S Meat Loaf is a family favorite. Lightly beat 2 eggs, add 1 pound ground beef, season with dash of oregano, thyme, salt and pepper. Add 1 7-1/2-ounce can sliced or chopped mushrooms and form into loaf. Place in baking dish and top with 7-1/2 ounce can tomato sauce and bake 50 minutes at 350.

KANAKA STEW

Want to make like the travelers of yore? Cure the pork or goat you bag! And it works equally well with fresh beef, too. Cut meat into chunks, sprinkle generously with Hawaiian salt and *lomi* it well. Line the bottom of a 5 gallon crock with layer of salt, place the meat in it, pack it down and cover with more salt and secure lid. The meat is preserved and ready for cooking in a month or when the brine covers the meat. It can stay unrefrigerated indefinitely.

Reach in and take what you want, wash off the salt, put in pot, boil about 5 to 10 minutes, throw out salty water and repeat until water is not too salty. . . maybe 2 or 3 times. Cook with scant water in covered pot with onions and cabbage for a good old *Kanaka Stew.*

BARBECUED SHORT RIBS

KIKUMI FUJITA'S Barbecued Short Ribs didn't last long at the church supper!

Take as much of the fat as possible off 3 pounds short ribs (or spare ribs or chicken) and marinate in following sauce: 1/2 C ketchup, 1/2 C soy, 3/4 T raw brown sugar (or white), dash of salt, jigger of sherry, small clove mashed garlic and finely chopped ginger according to your taste. Marinate the meats all day but if you're doing chicken leave it overnight and all day. Bake in 350 oven for 1 hour.

BEEF BURGUNDY

MAGGIE'S Beef Burgundy: Place 2 ounces of bacon at the bottom of the pot evenly. Add 1/2 pound carrots and 1/4 pound onions, the juice of 1 squeezed clove of garlic and 1 shallot. Add 2 pounds stewing beef and cover with 1/2 pound carrots and 1/4 pound onions, salt and pepper, 1 C brandy, 1-1/2 C burgundy and 2 C of broth. Cover all with 2 ounces of bacon. Cook on medium heat until it boils then lower heat to low for 2-1/2 hours. Serves 4.

GRILLED HAMBURGER VARIETIES

Grilled Hamburger Varieties:

Plain good ground beef with salt and pepper.

Ground beef combined with chopped white or green onions and seasoning.

Ground beef, grated garlic, ginger, finely chopped onions (green and white), soy to taste and pepper.

To stretch: To ground round add: per pound, 1 egg, 3 slices bread soaked in water and wrung dry, chopped onions, chopped parsley, ketchup, seasoning, mix all together and add just enough water to hold together.

SPAGHETTI

If your gang loves Spaghetti, try this one served with a green salad and hot buttered French bread and red wine for those who do! Boil 1/2 pound spaghetti in salted water until tender and drain. In frypan add 1 minced clove garlic to 2 T oleo and brown slightly. Add 2 pounds lean ground round and brown. Season. Add 1 16-ounce can sugar corn and number 2-1/2 can whole tomatoes and simmer five minutes stirring well. Add spaghetti and mix thoroughly. Put in buttered baking dish, cover with as much cream cheese broken in pieces as you like and bake in 350 oven for 1 hour!

VEAL AND EGGPLANT

Veal and Eggplant casserole is good served over buttered and parmessaned egg noodles. Saute a large chopped onion, 1 clove minced garlic, 3 T finely chopped green pepper, and 1 7-1/2-ounce can drained sliced mushrooms in 2 T olive oil until golden brown.

Stir in 2 6-ounce cans tomato sauce, pinch of oregano, 1 bay leaf, 1/2 t salt and 1/4 t pepper. Simmer 20 minutes.

Rub 1 pound 1/2-inch sliced veal cutlets with clove of garlic, dip in mixture of beaten egg and milk, then in fine dry bread crumbs, coating both sides well. Fry and brown meat in 4 T olive oil. Place over layers of par-boiled sliced eggplant in 12x8 baking dish and pour over sauce. Bake in 350 degree oven for 30 minutes. Place 1/2 pound or more sliced Mozarella cheese over meat and bake 5 minutes longer or until cheese melts and forms a good crust.

KALUA ROAST PORK

You have a choice with this Roast Pork Kalua Style. . . *pupus* or 'mini *luau*'. Thaw a 5-6 pound pork butt. . . it should have just enough fat so's not to dry out but not too greasy. Spread some *ti* leaves on a huge piece of heavy duty aluminum foil and place the butt in the middle. Score the fat in smallish cubes and sprinkle generously on all sides with Hawaiian salt and Liquid Smoke. Be sure and marinate the liquid into folds of meat and fat and especially the cubes. Wrap de-veined large *ti* leaves around the meat, pull up the foil around it and seal the bundle completely. Bake in 325 oven for at least 4-5 hours. Lay newspaper on counter, undo package, put butt back to broil in pyrex dish and pour over the juices from foil. Broil the fat for a few minutes to crispen. Cool and shred it in serving pieces like *kalua* pig for *luau*. For *pupus* cut into chunks bite-size and serve with tooth picks, Hawaiian salt and either dish of *poi* or cubes of cooked *taro*. The Liquid Smoke sauce is the most important ingredient!

CHOW MEIN

AH KAM WONG'S Chow Mein is a masterpiece of culinary and gastronomic art!

Mix 1 package wet noodles with 1 package bean sprouts and sprinkle 2 T oyster sauce over and warm in slow oven. Stir fry in following order: 1/2 pound sliced pork, 1 C sliced carrots, 1 C sliced round onions, 1 C sliced celery, 1 C *pepeiau*, 1 bundle broccoli chopped and last of all a package of Chinese peas (remove strings). Make gravy: 1 T cornstarch, 1 t sugar, 3 T soy sauce, add water to desired consistency and cook over low heat, mix with vegetables and pour over noodles. Garnish with Chinese parsley.

PORK CHOP SUEY

EMMA DE FRIES has an easy-quick Pork Chop Suey dish. Slice 1 pound lean pork thin as for chop suey. Simmer in pan with 1/2 C water and steam 4-5 minutes. Bring to a rolling boil, turn to low, throw in 4 cloves garlic chopped fine and continue steaming until water evaporates. Add 1-3 T soy and 2 C watercress and turn off the fire. Serve over rice. (The addition of sliced or quartered white onions is good, too.)

PORK HASH FILLING MIXTURE

From JANICE YEE'S kitchen is an all time favorite. She includes it in her book, *"The Fast Gourmet from Hawaii"*, but this is her old tattered recipe of years ago! Pork Hash Filling Mixture 1 pound pre cooked pork hash, 1/2 pound raw fishcake, 1/2 C water chestnuts, minced, 1/4 C finely minced ham, 3/4 C green onions, chopped fine or minced, 1/4 C Chinese parsley, 1 t ajinomoto, 1 t salt, 1 t shoyu. Mix all ingredients thoroughly, fill won ton pi squares and deep fry them, or steam until cooked to serve with cooked mustard cabbage and lots of rice.

Janice's latest addition calls for 20 large dried mushroom caps soaked in salt water with stems removed. Fill the softened mushrooms full of pork hash filling and place in pan and steam over boiling water for half an hour.

PICKLED PORK

Pickled Pork: Slice a 6 pound pork butt thin as for *teriyaki* and marinate in: 1 C brown sugar, 6 cloves crushed garlic, 1/2 C chili pepper, plus 6-8 small red Hawaiian chili peppers crushed. You might know better about the addition of peps! Marinate and keep turning in refrigerator for at least 4 days.

Grill over charcoal fire and serve between hamburger buns or with hot rice!!

BAKED PIG

RAYMOND SMITH has his pet way of cooking Baked Pig's Feet. Buy only front feet. Cut into serving size pieces. Blanch them. Drain and pour over them cold water. Mix 2 T flour, 2 T shoyu, 2 t salt and make a paste; smear on feet, let dry. In frying pan put some oil, fry ginger and garlic, squashed or pressed, until they are brown. Then into a pot put garlic and ginger, the pig's feet plus 1/2 C vinegar, 1/2 C water, 3/4 C sugar. Simmer for about an hour, or until feet are done. Get out your chopsticks and go to it!

TONGUE

You either adore Tongue or positively rise above it! Wash fresh tongue and simmer with water to cover, sliced onion, bay leaf, 2 T pickling spices, dill seed, stalk of chopped celery, leaves and all, slices of lemon, salt and pepper and forget about if for at least three hours or when the fork goes through tenderly. Remove from the liquid and peel. Amazingly enough tongue can be very fatty, too, so it's a good idea to refrigerate and lift the lard on this one, too. . . you'll be amazed.

ORIENTAL FLAVORED TONGUE

For an Oriental Flavored Tongue. . . slice in serving pieces and brown evenly in skillet with oil and as much garlic as you like but remember to remove. Drain off the fat when brown and add 1 to 2 C of the stock, and according to your own personal taste. . . soy, brown sugar, vinegar, grated ginger, five-spices and *sake*. Simmer gently until slices are well marinated. If you're too heavy on the soy, add more stock. Thicken if you like with cornstarch and water paste.

BEEF TONGUE IN WINE

Beef Tongue in Wine: Boil a fresh tongue in lightly salted water to cover for 1 hour, remove, skin and trim off roots. In oven proof casserole brown lightly 2 onions and 2 carrots cut in pieces in 1 T bacon fat or oleo. Add the prepared tongue, 1 clove garlic, 6 whole cloves, 6 crushed peppercorns, 1 t salt, 1 C dry white wine and 4 C of the water tongue was boiled in. Cook this tightly covered in 250 oven for 2 hours or until tender. Remove tongue, cool and store in refrigerator. Strain the broth then cool and store in refrigerator. Next day bring broth to boil and add 2 ounces brandy, simmer one minute and remove from heat. Slice the tongue and arrange in slices in serving dish, sprinkle with minced parsley, garnish with carrots, pour on the broth and serve either hot or cold.

KIMO AND SARAH WILDER'S home at the end of Kalia Road in Waikiki is now the site of the present Sheraton Hotel. It was here under the extensive *hau* arbor that they entertained so hospitably and here are two of Sarah's favorite entrees.

SMOKED TONGUE

Smoked Tongue: Boil tongue slowly for 4 hours turning occassionally, remove skin and root and place back in same water to cook another hour. Place in covered roasting pan and add 1 C brown sugar, 1 T whole cloves, 2 to 3 sticks cinnamon, 1 C raisins, 1 pint sherry and leave covered in slow oven 1 hour. Remove spices and serve with rice or noodles.

LAMB SHANKS

When Sarah made Lamb Shanks she never cut the bone.

Roll 6 shanks in seasoned flour until thoroughly coated then brown well in pan of hot oil. Place in baking dish, add 1 or more cloves minced garlic, 1 large onion sliced, salt and pepper, celery salt, poultry seasoning and sprinkle 1 package onion soup mix and 1/2 C water over and cover. Bake at 350 til meat begins to fall from bones. Add more water if it seems to be drying out.

LEG OF LAMB

NETTY HANSEN never seems to worry if she has unexpected company! She grabs a frozen leg of lamb out of the freezer, douses it with Worcestershire sauce and sprinkles it generously with garlic salt.

Roast in 375 oven for 1-1/2 hours or until the color you desire. . . some like it quite pink!

Or sprinkle a thawed leg of lamb generously with curry powder, garlic salt and powdered ginger. Roast according to your preference.

Baked bananas or papaya is good with this.

If you're making curry with the left-over lamb, be sure to remove gristle and skin and some fat before cutting in chunks to add to the sauce.

LIVER

Here's another either you do or you don't. . . Liver. Soak liver in pan of water with generous sprinkling of Hawaiian salt for about an hour. Remove skin and membrane, pat dry, squeeze juice of lemon over both sides, and lightly flour. Pre-heat oven to broil, and quickly broil liver dotted with butter on each side, adding more butter if needed. Takes about 5 minutes.

TRIPE

MRS. VALCINO CLARK LOPEZ'S Tripe is especially treasured by her daughter, Dolly Pang and she adds that it is better than any tripe dish she has ever had in Spain, France, Italy or Scotland!

Clean, blanch and cook in boiling water. . . always making sure that water covers the 3 pounds of beef honeycomb tripe. Reduce intensity to a slow penetrating simmer for approximately 6 hours until desired texture attained. Drain, cut in 2 inch or bite-size pieces. Transfer to saucepan, add 3 cans of chicken broth, 2 small cans tomato sauce, 2 clover garlic, minced, Hawaiian salt and white pepper to taste. . . and 1 large hand of grated fresh ginger (or to individual taste preference). But this is the key ingredient in this aromatic version. Simmer covered over low heat for approximately 45 minutes.

CHUTNEY MARINADE

An outstanding marinade for butterflied leg of lamb to grill over charcoal. Chutney Marinade: Combine chopped chutney and juice with grated ginger, minced garlic, 1 t or more curry powder, salt and pepper, lemon juice and oil for basting consistency. Let the leg marinate in this in securely tied plastic bag in refrigerator all afternoon then baste generously while broiling.

PARKER RANCH TERIYAKI SAUCE

Parker Ranch Teriyaki Sauce via chef SAL SALVADO at the Parker Ranch Kamuela Broiler. 1/2 C sugar, 2/3 C soy, 3 T sherry, 2 T oil, 2 T toasted sesame seeds, 1 stalk chopped green onions, 1/2 t salt, 1 T grated ginger, 1 crushed garlic clove, 1 T ajinomoto. Combine in covered jar and use to marinate steak before broiling.

STEAK SAUCE

Or try Kaaua Steak Sauce: 1 C red Hawaiian salt, 1 C raw brown sugar, 1 small can Coleman's mustard, bottle of garlic powder. Mix all together and keep in covered jar for handy use. Rub the mixture over grilled steak, slice and eat!

NEVER FAIL RIB ROAST

Never Fail Rib Roast: Preheat oven to 375 and cook roast 1 hour, turn off heat, seal oven and leave sign on door. . . *do not open.* One hour before serving cook at 300 for 50 minutes. Begin in morning and forget about it. This is for any size roast but be sure your meat is thawed.

LAMB CURRY

INDRU WATAMULL shares her Lamb Curry. Fry 3 finely chopped onions with enough oil in heavy bottom pan until brown. Add 2 pounds lamb (fat free, cut in 2 inch pieces), 1/2 T each tumeric, cumin, freshly chopped ginger, 2 T coriander and fry for 10 to 12 minutes. Add 1/4 t cayenne pepper, salt, 1 C yogurt and 2 ripe fresh tomatoes or equivalent canned without the juice.

Stir well and cook until all the moisture and yogurt have been dried. Cover and cook til meat is tender. Cook uncovered over very low heat for last 5 minutes.

SWEET AND SOUR PORK

CATHERINE DEAN'S Yankee version of Sweet Sour Pork is a great do-ahead. She leaves the proportions up to you. Saute sliced onions and bell pepper, add cubed pork steaks or butt and brown nicely. Add water to cover and grated ginger to taste. Simmer until pork is cooked. Add juice from a 2-1/2 ounce can pineapple chunks, brown sugar to taste, and thicken gravy with cornstarch mixed with some gravy. Simmer to cook thoroughly. Throw in pineapple chunks, just before serving.

....Seafood....

GIFTS FROM THE SEA
FISH

The Hawaiians of yore appreciated nature's gifts from the sea and felt as much at home in the ocean as a Californian does on the freeway. They feasted on fish, crustaceans, limpets, seaweed and harvested salt from natural beds in the lava. It was all there for the taking.

At today's prices, fish has become a great treat. So it behooves the housewife to cook fresh fish properly and investigate the merits of frozen and canned sea foods.

To be sure the fish is fresh. . . the eyes should be clear, gills red, the scales moist, and if possible poke the fish to see that the flesh is firm to the touch.

The most common method of cooking fish is frying. This takes more oil than meat and should be fried to a crisp outside and yet moist inside. Do not overcook fish as it tends to be dry. You may disguise a dry dark meat by soaking it in a sauce of soy, ginger, garlic and sugar to taste and then fry it. Or put thick chunks of marinated fish on skewers and grill it.

If you're broiling fish in the oven, be sure and brush it generously with butter or lay strips of bacon across to broil. You need not turn as the juices penetrate through the meat.

A mixture of vermouth, lemon juice and melted butter with seasonings of salt and pepper make a good marinade to baste grilled fish.

MULLET

Mullet is best for boiling. Simply cover the whole or cut-up fish with water, add some Hawaiian salt to taste, bring to a boil and simmer for a few minutes or until meat falls easily from the bones.

Steaming fish over boiling water takes a little more time but is the delicate way of cooking a good fish. The old timers simply added sliced round or green onions and sprinkled Hawaiian salt over to taste.

The true Hawaiian method of baking fish is to wrap it in *ti* leaves. Mullet, *Moi*, Red snapper or *weki* are all excellent for this. Clean the fish and sprinkle inside and out with salt, lay on clean wet *ti* leaves and wrap securely to keep the fish moist. You may want to add some sliced lemon and onion before wrapping. The Hawaiian rule of thumb is that when the juices of the fish seep out from the *ti* leaf bundle the fish is cooked.

FISH WITH COCONUT SAUCE

Fish with Coconut Sauce: Place 1-1/2 to 2 pounds of any white meat fish in baking pan, rub with Hawaiian salt and pour over it one can of thawed coconut cream. Baste several times during the cooking. . . 20 minutes per pound in moderate oven.

FISH WRAPPED IN LETTUCE LEAVES

Fish Wrapped in Lettuce Leaves. Sprinkle Hawaiian salt over 1-1/2 to 2 pound thick fillet of fresh *mahimahi* or any white fish, dribble some lemon juice over, and lay it on a bed of wet lettuce leaves. Place more leaves on top until the whole fillet is completely encased in clean lettuce leaves. Put it in a shallow pan in a 350 oven for 30-40 minutes or test for doneness. Scrape the leaves off the top but the bottom leaves with the fish drippings are delicious.

Instead of a regular Tartar Sauce to accompany this you mite want to try *avocado sauce*. Blend until smooth: 1 peeled, pitted and diced avocado, T vinegar, 3 T oil, 1 t lemon juice, salt and pepper.

TEMPURA STYLE FISH

GAIL CARSWELL'S Tempura Style Fish. Batter: beat together 1 C flour sifted with 1 pinch each baking powder and sugar, 1 C water, and 1 egg. Refrigerate for at least 15 minutes. Cut fish in about 1 inch chunks, fillet or slab, plop in batter and deep fry in sizzling oil to cook through and brown nicely.

FILLETS

FAYE'S Fillets: Sprinkle salt and pepper over either fillets or slab of fresh fish and let stand for 1/2 hour. Coat fish heavily with mayonnaise, place in pan and bake 30 minutes at 350 or until done, depending on thickness.

BAKED FISH

The STANLEY GRIEPS do a whole fish with mayonnaise but wrap it in *ti* leaves. Clean 1-2 pound fresh fish, rub inside and out with Hawaiian salt, place on ribbed *ti* leaves and slather with 1/2 C mayonnaise mixed with a splash of soy. Wrap leaves cross-wise and length-wise and wrap securely in foil. Bake 350 oven for one hour.

DRIED FISH

A fresh whole fish sprinkled generously with Hawaiian salt and put to dry in hot sun for a day or 2 keeps for weeks in covered jar. . . good *pupu*.

CRAB RICE CHEESE CASSEROLE

Crab-Rice-Cheese Casserole. Cook a C or 1-1/2 C of rice your way. Meanwhile hard cook 2 eggs and prepare the cheese sauce: melt 4 T butter in saucepan, stir in 3 T flour. Gradually add 1 C milk and cook while stirring until mixture is thick. Add 1 C shredded Cheddar cheese and stir until cheese is melted. Taste for seasoning. Continue cooking and stir in 1/2 C sherry or dry white table wine.

Dice hard-boiled eggs and combine rice, sauce and 1/2 pound or more of crab meat. Place in 2 quart buttered casserole and cover with shredded Cheddar cheese. Bake 30 minutes in 350 oven. Cook it longer if you like a crusty effect.

MACARONI SALMON CASSEROLE

Macaroni Salmon Casserole: Boil 7 ounces macaroni until tender, drain. Make some cream sauce or use a can of cream of mushroom soup then combine with macaroni and either 1 pound can of deboned salmon or 2 (7-ounce) cans tuna, place in buttered casserole, sprinkle ample bread crumbs and parmesan cheese or crushed potato chips for good crust. Bake to bubble.

MARINADE FOR FISH OR FOWL

Marinade for Fish or Fowl—ANITA STUCKY'S own specialty: Mix together well and marinate either shrimp or chicken 2 to 3 hours or longer: 1/2 C peanut oil, 2 large cloves crushed garlic, 3 T vinegar, 1 t salt, 6 T chili sauce, 2 handfuls chopped parsley, 2 t mixi-pep (hot sauce) and 3 T black pepper. Especially delicious when charcoal broiled!

LOMI SALMON

Lomi Salmon is a good *poi* supper item to introduce the *malihini* to *poi* as the *poi* soothes the saltiness! Don't ever add chopped onions to it. . . let the guests do this. Skin a good belly piece of salt salmon, about a pound, and cut in cubes. Soak in water for at least 3-4

hours, changing occasionally. Be sure it's not too salty before you add the tomatoes, but if you discover it is later just add more tomatoes. Wash and skin at least a dozen or more ripe, firm tomatoes. Shred the salmon with your fingers so as to remove all bones and gristle. Then *'lomi'* in the tomatoes with your fingers and mash and mix thoroughly to blend. Remove any pith or core, and remember one bad tomato can sour the whole dish! Keep in cool part of refrigerator and serve cold. You may freeze left-overs.

SQUID AND LUAU

Squid and Luau is another *poi* supper favorite. After cleaning the squid by removing the teeth and *ala ala* (ink bags) rinse well and pound vigorously with salt until tender. Boil in 2 C water and 1 t salt for 1/2 hour, drain, cut into serving pieces and combine with cooked *luau* leaves (or chopped spinach thawed and completely drained) and add can of thawed frozen coconut milk.

KEGEREE

Kegeree is a great dish for left-over fish. Melt 4 T butter in pan and add 3 C cold cooked fish and 1-1/2 C cooked rice. Cover and warm slowly turning to brown evenly on bottom. Serve with thin cream sauce and diced hard boiled eggs with generous sprinkling of chopped parsley.

TAHITIAN RAW FISH

Tahitian Raw Fish the Hawaiian Way! Cut fresh white fish into small cubes or slices. Cover completely with lime juice and let stand for several hours. . . the lime cooks the fish. Pour off juice and cover with coconut milk, salt and check taste. You may like the addition of finely sliced onions. . . suit yourself and guests!

JAPANESE RAW FISH OR SASHIMI

Japanese Raw Fish or Sashimi: Cut fish diagonally into slices 2 inches long and about 1/8 unch thick. Place on bed of shredded lettuce and chill. Serve with sauce made of soy, grated ginger and hot mustard to taste.

TARTAR SAUCE

GAIL CARSWELL'S Original Tartar Sauce: Combine to taste and consistency: chopped Kosher pickles, dill weed, diced onion and mayonnaise.

For a color change add beet juice to your regular mixture for tartar sauce. . . mayonnaise, lemon juice, chopped green onions and relish.

SOUR CREAM FISH BAKE

SYLVIA PABLO'S Sour Cream Fish Bake is a masterpiece to behold and taste! Cut up 3 pounds *mahimahi* or *ulua* into serving pieces. Wash and pat dry. Place in shallow baking dish, pour 1 C sherry over and marinate for 15 minutes on each side.

Discard juice, pour 1/4 C melted butter over fish and sprinkle with 1/2 t each salt and aji and 1/4 t pepper. Broil for 10 minutes and baste with pan juices. Set aside to cool slightly.

Mix 1/2 can cream of shrimp soup with 1/2 C each sour cream, chopped round onion and tiny shrimps. Spoon on top of fish and sprinkle with chopped macadamia nuts and paprika. Bake in 250 oven for 30 minutes.

If your're artistic you can shape and color it with paprika to resemble a fish.

ONO FISH SAUCE

KARL STEINGER'S Ono Fish Sauce is a cinch to make and can be stored in the refrigerator to use with other meats, too.

Boil 1-1/2 C water with a clove of minced garlic, 2 cubes beef bouillon, 1/4 slice lemon, shakes of salt and nutmeg.

Melt 1 T butter until golden brown and combine with the water. Thicken with 2/3 T cornstarch mixed to a smooth paste with 1/4 C water. Boil this all up, keep warm, and pour over fried fish. You don't even miss the tartar sauce.

Dip your fish fillets in beaten egg white and coat with very fine bread crumbs. Either let it set to dry or fry immediately. It browns beautifully in heated butter and so *ono*!

TANGY MAHIMAHI

Tangy Mahimahi: Grease shallow oblong baking dish with oleo, place 6 to 8 ounces per person of *mahimahi* fillets in dish, dab with ounce of oleo, 2 T lemon juice and 3 to 4 T sweet pickle relish. Bake in 350 oven for 15 to 20 minutes in center of oven. Do not turn or overcook fish. *Mahimahi* will become tough. Fish is done when a fork inserted into thickest part of fish causes it to flake easily.

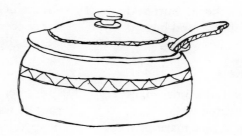

....Casseroles....

**THE COOK IS IN THE PARLOR. . .
CASSEROLES**

Don't be a "Jumping-Jack" host! Relax! Sit and enjoy your guests. Let the morning's labors or a thawed casserole put the joy into entertaining.

There's no need for slaving over a hot stove by yourself in the kitchen during the frivolities. Think casseroles and just look pretty and join the fun.

HAMBURGER-MACARONI DISH

Hamburger-Macaroni Dish: Saute 2 medium onions, finely chopped and 1 chopped green pepper in a little oleo till somewhat softened. Add 1 pound very lean hamburger and cook til red has gone. Add 1 28-ounce can tomatoes, chopping up so evenly mixed. Season with salt and pinch of sugar. Add 1 C *uncooked* macaroni, and 1/2 pound extra sharp cheddar cheese. Stir all in and check for seasoning. Bake in 300 oven for about an hour, til macaroni is of desired softness. Add more tomatoes if you think the combination is too stiff and pour off any fat after simmering meat.

BEEF CHUNKS IN SOUR CREAM

Beef Chunks in Sour Cream: Cut 3 pounds lean stewing beef in 1 inch cubes. Roll in flour and brown in 3 T fat. Add 2 medium onions sliced thinly and brown. Add 1-1/2 C sour cream, 2 C mushrooms, sliced, 1/2 t oregano, 1/4 t basil, 1 T salt and 1-1/2 t paprika. Put in casserole covered and bake 2 or more hours til meat is tender. Start at 350, after an hour or so reduce to 300. Serve with rice or noodles and it should do 6-8.

MEAT AND CHEESE CASSEROLE

Meat and Cheese Casserole: Cook 8-ounce package noodles in boiling water, drain and set aside. Fry and brown 1-1/2 pounds chopped beef in 1 T butter and add 2 8-ounce cans tomato sauce, 8-ounce package cream cheese, 1/2 pound mushrooms, 1 C cottage cheese, 1/2 C sour cream, 1/2 C chopped green onions, and 1 T chopped green pepper. Mix well. Combine mixture with noodles and bake in buttered casserole in 350 oven until bubbly and heated through.

SPINACH AND ARTICHOKES

Spinach and Artichokes: Cook 3 packages frozen chopped spinach as directed on package. Drain well and spread over 2 jars marinated artichokes (drained slightly) in 1-1/2 quart casserole. Beat 1 (8-ounce) package cream cheese, 4 T butter and 6 T milk and spread over spinach and artichokes. Dust with pepper and 1/2 C parmesan cheese. Refrigerate for 24 hours! Bake covered for 40 minutes in 375 oven. Great with baked chicken.

POI STEW

Poi Stew: Brown 3 pounds chuck or stew beef cut in 2-inch cubes in 1 T oil, cover with water and cook slowly 1-1/2 hours, add 2 round onions quartered, 1 C small tomatoes, fresh or canned, and salt to taste. Cook 1/2 hour longer. Use 1/2 C *poi* to thicken stew. Serve.

CHICKEN AND NOODLES CASSEROLE

Chicken and Noodles Casserole: Cook your chicken and de-bone and cut into bite-size pieces. Line the bottom of a casserole with lots of those dry noodles. . . large round package wrapped in cellophane. Alternate, cream of chicken soup, chicken pieces, chopped white and green onions, green pepper, celery, mushrooms, water chestnuts, sprinkle with salt and pepper and cover with soup. Pack down with a layer of more crisp noodles, cover and bake 350 oven for 1 hour then uncovered for 10 minutes.

AVOCADO CREPES WITH SHRIMP CASSEROLE

Avocado Crepes with Shrimp Casserole. *Crepes:* To 1/2 C mashed avocado add 4 eggs, 1/2 C flour, 1/4 t salt, 1/2 C milk and 1 to 2 T water. With a whisk blend mixture until smooth. Griddle up about 10-12 crepes.

Filling: Melt 2 T butter and stir in 3 T flour. Gradually add 1-1/2 C heated milk and stir constantly until sauce begins to thicken. Add 2 ounces diced Swiss cheese and cook until melted. Remove from heat and stir in 1/2 t Worcestershire sauce, salt and pepper to taste and 1 pound shrimp.

Place portion of the filling on each crepe and fold, arrange in single layer in well greased baking dish, sprinkle with 3 ounces grated Swiss cheese and dot with 1/4 C butter. Bake 400 oven for 10 to 15 minutes until hot and cheese is melted. Serve immediately. These crepes may be prepared in advance and frozen before baking. Wrap dish in freezer foil and freeze. Bake, wrapped in foil, in hot oven 400 for 15 minutes. Remove foil and bake uncovered 15 minutes longer.

RICE SPECIAL TUNA CASSEROLE

MARTHA ANN RICE'S Special Tuna Casserole is a specialty at Sunday lunches at Kukaiau Ranch on Hawaii.

Combine 4 cans cream of mushroom soup, 8 (7 ounce) cans drained tuna, 2 (13-1/2 ounce) cans evaporated milk, 2 (7-1/2 ounce) cans sliced and drained mushrooms, 2 small jars pimientos, 2-1/2 (9-ounce) cans shoe-string potatoes, and mix all up together.

Pour into large casserole and sprinkle 1/2 can of shoe-string potatoes over. Bake to bubble and heat through in 350 oven. Garnish with chopped parsley to serve.

Martha Ann is used to cooking for larger groups a la plantation life so she keeps a large plastic bucket solely for mixing the likes of large casseroles, tossed salads, potato salads or whatever.

EGG DISH

Kamaaina ladies adored going to SARAH WILDER'S at Waikiki for luncheon and finding her own special Sarah's Egg Dish for luncheon.

Add 1-1/2 t salt to 1 quart of cream and mix well. Pour in 8 ramekins, drop raw egg into each and cover with grated cheddar cheese.

Place them in flat pan half filled with water and bake until cheese is melted and browned. . . don't let the water in pan bubble.

She usually served a crispy, cold green salad with this and popovers.

DAD'S CHILI

Having the gang over for dinner and want to enjoy the party, too? You can do just this with Dad's Chili concocted by KARL GEO-RGE KOELLMANN. He dubs it a three pot method and makes it the day before the feast.

Pot 1 (the largest pan you have):

Soak 3 pounds pimento beans overnite, then wash several times and drain. Put in the big pot and cover with sufficient water.

Throw in 2 to 3 diced onions, salt and pepper and 3 garlic cloves per pound of beans. Boil at low heat then simmer gently until tender.

Keep stirring to keep the beans from sticking to the bottom and add more water if necessary. Simmer about 3 hours.

Pot 2: De-bone and trim all fat off of 5 pounds of T-bone or chuck or other lean meat and cut into small chunks. Do likewise to 6 large pork chops or steaks.

Brown meat together slowly, add seasoning and 1 large diced onion. Turn off heat when done.

Pot 3: Combine 1 round onion, diced; 1 can (28 ounces) whole tomatoes cut up; 5 cans (4-ounces) diced green chili, mild or hot (remove seeds if you don't want too hot); 5 cloves pressed garlic; boil covered to bring flavor and heat out. Keep simmering.

Add *Pot 3* to the beans and the following: 1 T cumin, 2 T oregano, 3 T red chili powder (or more), salt and pepper and 2 (8-ounce) cans tomato paste. Be sure and rinse out these cans well into the sauce.

Add *Pot 2* to bean and chili pot and simmer it all for 1 to 2 hours. Test seasoning and if not hot enough add tabasco, cayenne or hot sauce.

Serve in big bowls with crackers and milk or beer, depending on the crowd. Serves about 40 people but freezes very well.

MACARONI AND BEEF CASSEROLE

Macaroni and Beef Casserole: In skillet brown 1/2 pound each lean ground beef and bulk pork sausage and 1 medium onion chopped. Drain fat, add 1 6-ounce can tomato paste, 1 C water, 1/2 t oregano, 1/2 t salt and simmer 5 minutes. In 2-1/2 quart casserole layer 2 C cooked elbow macaroni, half the meat, sauce and 1/2 C shredded sharp cheddar cheese. Repeat and top with lots of grated cheddar cheese. Bake 375 oven 20-25 minutes. . . 6 servings.

A LA PITTMAN

Osso Bucco a la Pittman: Cut 2 veal shanks into three pieces, roll in flour and brown in a little oil on all sides. Add C each water and white wine. Cover and simmer 20 minutes. Muddle clove garlic, 1/2 t basil, 3 or 4 tomatoes, 2 medium onions cut up and 1 sprig parsley minced; simmer two hours. Place in casserole and warm for dinner.

BAKED CORNED BEEF

Baked Corned Beef: Pull out enough aluminum foil to wrap a piece of corned beef. Sprinkle with pickling spices, add sliced or quartered onion, 1 sliced orange, peel and all, and 2 stalks of celery. Add about 1/4 C water and fold carefully to seal. Place in pan in 300 oven and bake for 3 hours. You don't lose the juices. Cook potatoes and carrots separately and throw in cabbage last minute to par cook for crunch, or have cold slaw for salad.

FANCY COMPANY CASSEROLE

True to her word, HARRIET WARREN sent the recipe for a 'simple buffet supper' for 12 she was whipping up after the last Daughters of Hawaii meeting.

Fancy Company Casserole: Combine 2 pounds ground beef, 1/2 C sour cream, 3 T dried onion soup mix, 1 egg slightly beaten and 1-1/2 C soft bread crumbs and shape into 16 balls. Brown in 1/4 C butter. Add 1 (8-ounce) can mushrooms undrained, 1 (10-ounce) can cream of chicken soup and 1-2/3 C water. Simmer for 20 minutes. Place in 3-quart casserole.

BUTTER CRUMB DUMPLINGS

Butter Crumb Dumplings: Mix 2 C sifted flour, 4 t baking powder, 1 T poppy seed, 1 t each celery salt and poultry seasoning, and 2 t dried onion flakes.

Blend in 1/4 C oil and 3/4 C plus 2 T milk for dough. Stir 1/4 C melted butter into 2 C soft bread crumbs.

Drop dough by T into 12 equal portions into buttered crumbs; roll to cover with crumbs. Place on top of casserole. Bake at 400 for 20-25 minutes or until dumplings are golden. This should be ample for 8. . . so double, triple or whatever.

ITALIAN DELIGHT

And from the files of the late PHOEBE FITGERALD comes 2 super casserole dishes. She served her scrumptious Italian Delight with garlic bread and a gorgeous green salad right from the garden. Like all good cooks Phoebe always apologized and said, "Sorry can't give you definite quantities of ketchup, Worcestershire, salt etc. as I do it by taste after it's hot. That way. . . taste, add, taste, add or not as you see fit! Sometimes 'Twink' gets to it and adds a dollop of wine. . . not bad either. Make it in huge quantities as it freezes well right in the casserole, just don't put the cheese on it until it is heated through again and ready to eat."

Italian Delight: Boil 1 package of chow fun noodles (not egg) but don't overcook. Fry 1 pound hamburger, 1 medium onion, chopped, 1 clove garlic, chopped in a little oil. Add to casserole with noodles, 1 can whole kernel corn, 1 can sliced mushrooms or more if you like, 1 can tomato sauce, season. . . being generous with ketchup and Worcestershire sauce. Taste and add what is needed.

Heat covered in 350 oven til bubbly. Then cover top generously with 1/2 pound grated cheddar cheese. Put back in oven uncovered until cheese melts. *Ono!*

CHICKEN CASSEROLE

And her Chicken Casserole is special, too. Mix all together and refrigerate over night: 2 C each diced cooked chicken and cooked rice, 1/3 C chopped almonds, 2 cans cream of mushroom soup, 1 C mayonnaise, 1/2 C chopped onions, 2 chopped hard boiled eggs, 1-1/2 C diced celery, 2 T lemon juice, 1/2 t salt and 1 small can water chestnuts, sliced.

Before baking cover top with crushed potato chips and bake 1 hour in 350 oven.

GROUND ROUND CASSEROLE

MELINDA WHITE'S Ground Round Casserole freezes beautifully and a great do-ahead. In a large baking pan layer the following in order: well drained, cooked, chopped spinach;

crumbled hamburger in basic tomato or spaghetti sauce, cooked noodles; mixture of 1/2 cream cheese and 1/2 sour cream with chopped green onions. Top with generous sprinkling of grated sharp cheddar cheese and bake at 350 for 30 minutes uncovered.

WELA KA HAO CHILI

ARTHUR AKINA'S Wela Ka Hao Chili will separate the boys from the men! In a very large saucepan, heat 2 T cooking oil and 1 T Hawaiian salt over a medium high burner. Add 2 large round onions, minced, and 3 large cloves garlic, minced. Cook until tender.

Push aside and crumble 2 pounds lean ground round into pot and stir 4 to 5 minutes. Add 1 t cumin seed, 2 to 3 T chili powder, 2 T oregano and stir all into meat and onions, cooking til meat just looses pink coloring.

Add 6 cans chili with beans, 4 cans chili without beans (hot), 1/2 can hot water and stir all together. Lower heat and let simmer uncovered 15 minutes.

Add 2 T dry, flaked hot Mexican chili pepper and stir it in. Check seasoning for sufficient salt, chili powder, chili pepper and oregano. Simmer uncovered additional 1/2 hour. Cook and refrigerate over night. Warm to serve.

SWISS ENCHILADAS

CYNTHIA GRANT'S Swiss Enchiladas are supreme. Cook, debone, and cut into strips 2 whole chicken breasts. Combine with following mixture: 4-ounce can diced green chilis, 1 C sour cream, 1/2 C chopped green onions, 1/2 small can chopped ripe olives, 1/2 t salt and 2 or 3 t green taco sauce.

Fry 12 tortillas, one at a time about 30 seconds until limp. Dip in 2 C whipping cream, fill with chicken mixture, roll up and place close together in 9x13 inch pan.

Pour remaining cream over enchiladas, cover all with 1-1/2 C shredded Jack cheese. Bake in 350 oven 20 minutes or until bubbly and cheese is melted. 6-8 servings.

HEARTY BEEF CASSEROLE

Hearty Beef Casserole: Saute 1/2 C finely chopped onions, 2 minced cloves of garlic, and 1 pound sliced mushrooms in 1/4 pound butter until lightly browned.

Add 2 pounds ground round and cook until red color disappears. Stir in 8 T burgundy wine, 4 T lemon juice, 2 cans consomme and salt and pepper to taste. Simmer uncovered for 15 minutes and stir in 1/2 pound uncooked thinnest noodles you can find. Cook covered 5 minutes or until noodles are tender.

Mix in 2 C sour cream, sprinkle with lots of minced parsley and keep in oven to bubble and melt.

SOUR CREAM ENCHILADA

BERYL MOIR'S Sour Cream Enchilada is a popular dish for small dinner parties served with a salad of artichoke hearts, Mandarin oranges, lettuce and a tart dressing.

Steam and debone a 3 pound chicken.

Combine: 5 cans cream of chicken soup, 2 C sour cream, 1 4-ounce cans green chilis chopped, 2 C Jack cheese grated, 2 C grated Cheddar and mix well.

Add chicken to half of this mixture. Spread 12 flour tortillas with this, roll up, lay

in casserole and pour over remaining sauce. Sprinkle 1 C grated cheddar cheese over all and bake in 350 oven 35-45 minutes uncovered.

....Desserts....

THOSE EXTRA POUNDS. . .
COOKIES, PUDDING, CAKES, PIES, ETC.

All of us have a sweet tooth. . . some more than others. Some can afford to have and some can't. You can go for weeks without serving desserts at your house but when company comes it's the signal to oblige with a 'make-up-for-lost-pounds-binge' and hang the calories.

Junkets and fruit flavored gelatins used to be like sentinels in the refrigerator. . . standing there in little individual cups and ready at all times. But now they're mostly used as just a base for bigger and better things.

However, there are still those large jars of fresh cookies around!

GROVE FARM SUGAR COOKIES

Cream 2 C brown-washed sugar with 1/2 C butter. Add 2 beaten eggs, 1 t vanilla. Sift in 2-3/4 C flour and 1 t soda. Mix well, shape into rolls, wrap in wax paper and leave overnight in ice box. Cut 1/4 inch thick and bake in 350 oven for 15 minutes.

NEW ENGLAND COCONUT COOKIES

Cream 1/2 C shortening, 1/2 C granulated sugar, 1/2 C brown sugar well before adding 1 unbeaten egg.

Sift 1-1/2 C flour with 1/2 t each baking powder, salt and soda. Combine with 1 C quick oatmeal, 1 C shredded coconut and 1/4 t vanilla. Add to shortening mixture, mix well, and drop on cookie sheet by teaspoonfuls. Bake at 350 until brown.

EASY COOKIES

STEPHANIE ELLIS whips up these Easy Cookies anytime. Mix 1 box of any flavored cake mix with 1/2 pint of sour cream. Drop by teaspoon on cookie sheet. Bake at 350 about 10 minutes.

LEMON SQUARES

DORIS KAWAKI'S contribution to her church recipe book collection was Lemon Squares.

Crust: Mix 1 C butter, 2 C flour and 1/2 C chopped nuts. Press into bottom of 9x13 inch pan, bake 400 oven for 15 minutes.

First Layer: Beat 1 C sifted powdered sugar, and 1 softened package 8-ounce cream cheese. Add 1 C non-dairy whipped topping. Spread on baked crust and refrigerate.

Second Layer: Mix together and pour over set cream mixture: 2 packages (3-1/2 ounces) lemon instant pudding, 3 C cold milk and 1 T grated lemon peel. Refrigerate until set. Top with whipped cream. *(Island Ideas Cook Book)*

EASY BROWNIES

ALICE HIRANO is a busy working lady so was delighted to find Easy Brownies something simple and pleasing to her family.

In 9x13x2-1/2 inch baking pan melt 1 block oleo on top of stove. Remove from heat, mix in 2 C brown sugar and cool thoroughly before adding 2 eggs. Mix well.

Add 1 t vanilla and gradually add 2 C flour sifted with 2 t baking powder. Stir in 1 C each chocolate chips, grated coconut, chopped nuts, and mix thoroughly. Level out in pan and bake 350 oven for 20-30 minutes. Cool and cut in squares.

KISSES

Beat 2 egg whites until stiff, gradually add 2/3 C sugar and pinch of cream of tartar while beating. Add 1 t vanilla and fold in 1 6-ounce package chocolate mint bits and 1 t oil of peppermint or vanilla. Drop from tablespoon on 2 cookie sheets lined with paper.

Preheat oven to 350. . . and here's the punch line. Turn off the oven when heated, put the sheets in the oven, close the door, go

to bed and the next morning you'll find the most delectable surprise to nibble on all day.

"Send 'Honey' off with a big kiss to really start his day," says NANCY PITTMAN of Belvedere, CA.

PUFF RICE SQUARES

Here's GLADYS BORRERO'S coveted recipe for Puff Rice Squares.

Heat 6 C puff rice and 1/3 C halved peanuts in 9x13 inch pan in 250 oven.

In a big pot over low heat melt 1/2 block each oleo and butter and 1 C sugar. Stir frequently, don't let butter burn and watch for at least 15 minutes. Gladys underlined low heat and slowly!

When the combination turns taffy colored and carmelizes then work *fast*. Dump in warm puff rice and peanuts and mix well. Put back into 9x13 pan and tap lightly with bottom of coffee mug to flatten. . .gently! Cool 10 minutes and cut into squares. Store in tightly covered can.

LEMON CAKE TOP PUDDING

Lemon Cake Top Pudding created quite a response amongst the ladies and for sure this is in most everyone's files. . . but for those who don't have it here it is.

This is MRS. FRANK E. WALTON'S recipe that has been in one family for 150 years.

Mix 1 T butter, 3/4 C sugar and 2 T flour. Add 2 egg yolks, 1/4 C lemon juice and 1 C milk. Fold in two beaten egg whites.

Bake 35 minutes at 375 in unbuttered dish set in pan of water. Or this can be baked in an unbaked pie crust. Serve with whipped cream.

WINONA SEARS suggested favoring home-grown pruducts by subbing *lilikoi* juice for the lemons. Try it, it's delicious!

BANANA DESSERT

Either bake or slowly fry really ripe bananas in butter or oleo until soft and cooked. Put into casserole or individual dishes, dot with butter, pour over guava jelly, dollops of rum and serve hot with whipped cream.

CABINET PUDDING

Cabinet Pudding is a great way to use up left-over cake. Cut up or crumble stale sponge or fruit cake and line a buttered pie dish. Sprinkle currants or sultanas over sponge cake.

Make a custard with 1/2 pint hot milk and 1 beaten egg. Pour over cake. Leave to stand few minutes than bake until custard sets.

CHOCOLATE PUDDING

Like Chocolate Pudding? How's about Italian style? Add to homemade or packaged chocolate pudding while cooking: 2 T dry sherry, 1 t lemon juice and few slivers of lemon peel. Pour into your fancy dessert dishes and chill. Serve with whipped cream if company is coming.

APPLESAUCE MACAROON PUDDING

FRANCIE HAINSE'S Appleasuce Macaroon Pudding is simple and delicious, too. Line bottoms of dessert bowls with macaroons. Sprinkle with ample sherry and fill with applesauce. Top with sour cream or at the last minute before serving. . . vanilla ice cream.

GUINDIN

FATIMA CAMERON'S Guindin may some day take the place of *haupia*. Combine meat of 2 grated coconuts and 1 pound sugar in bowl. Let stand 2 hours. Add 1 cube melted oleo and 10 eggs, 2 at a time, beating well after each addition.

Pour into mini-muffin tins buttered and sugared. Place in tray of hot water in 350 oven for 40 minutes, cool and turn upside down. Makes 36 tarts, which keep for several days in the refrigerator.

APPLE CRISP

VIRGINIA GILL is true to her mother-in-law's Apple Crisp. In square pan combine and mix 1 large can Comstock apples, 1 C sugar and 1/2 t cinnamon. Pour over following mixture: break 1 egg into 1 C each sugar and flour sifted with 1/4 t salt, 1 t baking powder and stir until crumbly.

Dot with nuts, bake 375 for 1/2 hour and serve hot or cold, with or without cream or ice cream.

SEEDLESS GRAPES

LORI PANTALEO'S Seedless Grapes is a simple but elegant dessert and everyone loves it. Combine enough sour cream and tiny pieces of chopped candied dried ginger to really coat and marinate de-stemmed seedless grapes.

Cover and refrigerate for 2 days. Serve with your best cookies.

KANTEN

DOROTHY SAITO'S Kanten is a good gelatin dessert to bring out for a change. Rinse

4 red *agar-agar* sticks and tear into 1 inch pieces. Soak in 8 C water for 30 minutes then bring to a boil. Add 3 C sugar stirring constantly while continuing to boil for 30-40 minutes. . . . watching for 'boiling over'. Add 3 drops cinnamon extract (or 40 cinnamon hard candies and lessen sugar about 1/2 C). Pour into 7x11 inch pan, cool, and cut into desired shapes for serving.

GUAVA ICE

JANET BELL'S Guava Ice is money in the bank for unexpected company. Mix together: 2 C guava puree, 2 T lime or lemon juice, 1 C sugar or more if guavas are very sour, 3 T Pream dissolved in 1/2 C warm water. Stir well and freeze. When mushy, beat and return to freezer.

QUICK CAKE FROSTING

Mix up a carton of sour cream with a box of confectionary powdered sugar and 2 C thawed frozen shredded coconut. Mix well and frost plain cake.

CARMEL SAUCE FOR ICE CREAM

Combine and cook slowly over low heat or better yet in a double boiler. . . 2 C brown sugar, 1 C cream, 1 cube (1/4 pound) butter and slivered almonds. Keep warm for serving.

STRAWBERRY ICE BOX CAKE FILLING

JANE NAKASHIMA'S Strawberry Ice Box Cake Filling evaporated at the church potluck supper!

Heat 1 carton thawed frozen strawberries with syrup and 1/2 C sugar. Add 1 box strawberry jello, stir well and add 1 package gelatin dissolved in 1/4 C water. Mix and cool.

Whip 1 frozen (13 ounce) can evaporated milk and fold into cooled strawberry mixture. Place slices of pound cake (1-1/2 cakes) in buttered 9x13 cake pan, cover with layer of filling, layer of sliced cake, and top with filling.

Frost with whipped cream and chill until set and ready to serve.

ASPARAGUS CHEESE CAKE

From her book, *"All You Want to Know About Asparagus"*, NANCY HEWITT suggests Asparagus Cheese Cake for starters. Combine the following and mix well: 2 pounds ricotta cheese, 2 C smooth asparagus puree, 8 eggs, 2/3 C sugar, 1/4 C unbleached flour, 1/4 C heavy cream, 2 T grated orange rind, 2 T vanilla extract and a dash of ground nutmeg.

Pour into an oiled and floured 8-inch spring form pan and bake 375 oven for 50-60 minutes. Let cool before removing ring form.

Serve with *Mandarin Orange Sauce*. Puree 1 (11-ounce) can drained mandarin orange segments in blender and add 1 T confectioners' sugar and blend well. Or you may sub with orange flavored whipped cream. This cake keeps for several days in the refrigerator. . . if you don't finish it off at the first sitting.

CHEESECAKE

NANCY'S Cheesecake. . . "The best you ever ate, and it is a large cake!"

Crust: Crush and mix in 1-3/4 C graham crackers, 3 T brown sugar, 1 t cinnamon and 3 T butter melted. Press in bottom of 10 inch spring form pan.

Cake: Cream and mix well 3 softened (8-ounce) packages cream cheese with 1-1/2 C sugar. Keep mixing well while adding 1 pint sour cream and 1 pint heavy whipping cream. Then add 4 eggs blending well after each. Mix in 1/2 t vanilla and 2 T lemon extract. Pour into crust.

Bake one hour at 350 in preheated oven. Turn off oven. Do not open to peek. Leave in oven overnight, refrigerate in morning and serve at dinner!

TOMATO SOUP CAKE

BETTY SCOTT'S Tomato Soup Cake: Combine and let stand: 1 can tomato soup and 1 t baking soda.

Combine 1/2 C melted butter, 1 C sugar, 1 t each cinnamon, nutmeg and vanilla. Add soup and soda mix alternately with 2 C flour and mix until smooth. Add 1/2 C light raisins and 1 C broken walnuts and mix well. Pour in greased and floured oblong pan and bake in 350 oven for 45-50 minutes or until straw inserted in center comes out clean. May be served plain or with powdered sugar icing.

PUMPKIN PIE CAKE

NANCY TESHIMA, a Kauai school teacher, divides her time between the class room, her garden and her kitchen. Nancy's Pumpkin Pie Cake either fills 2 baked pie shells or can be baked in 8x13 inch pan.

Crust: Cream 1-1/2 block margarine or butter with 1-1/2 C flour, 3 T confectioners sugar and add 1/2 C chopped walnuts. It will be dry and crumbly so you have to press and

spread this mixture down on the bottom of pan. Bake in 425 oven for 8 to 10 minutes, but if you think it still looks a little white, turn off the heat and leave it in a few more minutes. Cool and proceed with the filling.

Pumpkin Filling: In caucepan, combine 3 envelopes gelatin, 1-1/2 C brown sugar (firmly packed), 1 t each salt and cinnamon and 1-1/2 C water. Stir well and bring to boil and remove from burner.

Spoon in 1 quart vanilla ice cream and stir until it melts. Then add a 2-1/2 size can of pumpkin and mix until smooth. Chill until filling starts to jell, then pour into pie shell and chill until firm.

CHERRY CAKE

JEANNE TOULON whips up this Cherry Cake with ease then sits back and smiles at all the compliments.

Line a 9x13 inch pan with 2 cans of cherry pie filling. Melt 1 cube butter and mix into contents of 1 box of white cake mix. Sprinkle on top of the cherry mix. Sprinkle this with as much chopped walnuts as you like and bake in 350 oven 30 to 40 minutes or until golden brown.

FRESH PAPAYA SAUCE CAKE

MAX T. MORI, the famous chef at Kona Inn many years ago, used another method for Fresh Papaya Sauce Cake. Stew 1 C very ripe diced papaya (or mango) with 3 T water for 20 minutes. Sieve and save the liquid.

Sift 3 times 1 T baking powder, 1/2 T salt, 1/3 t each cinnamon and nutmeg, 1/4 t each mace and ginger, and 1-1/2 C flour.

Cream 1/4 C shortening and 1 C sugar until fluffy and add 1 well beaten egg. Add flour alternately with papaya liquid, fold in 1 T lemon juice and 1/2 C raisins. Bake in 325 oven for 45 minutes.

PUMPKIN PIE

BETSY NAKAMURA'S Pumpkin Pie Cake is so rich and delicious that you really should cut in small pieces.

Blend and mix well: 1 large (1 pound 13 ounce) can pumpkin, 1 (13 ounce) can evaporated milk, 3 eggs, 1 t nutmeg, 1/2 t each ginger, cloves, salt, 2 t cinnamon and 1-1/2 C sugar.

Pour into greased 9x13 pan and sprinkle over 1 box yellow cake mix (dry). Gently pat down with spoon and sprinkle 1 C chopped walnuts over, drizzle 2 sticks melted butter over all and bake at 350 for 50 minutes. Cool and cut in squares.

KAMUELA PRUNE CAKE

EVA KELAMAKIA learned the art of cake making from her mother, Maryann Lincoln Lindsey who thought nothing of baking 20 cakes beginning Friday evening for a Saturday party. The cakes were done to perfection in her trusty kerosene oven. Here is her famous Kamuela Prune Cake which won first prize at the County Fair.

Cream 1 block butter with 1 C sugar until fluffy. . . really fluffy! Add 3 beaten egg yolks and beat. Add 1 C chopped stewed prunes pitted and thoroughly drained.

Sift 2 C flour with 1 t each nutmeg, cloves, baking powder, and 2 t baking soda and add alternately to butter mixture with 1 C prune juice.

Mix thoroughly and fold in three stiffly beaten egg whites. Bake in two round layer pans at 350 for 40-50 minutes. Cool and frost with 7 minute frosting combined with one C mashed prunes.

CHOCOLATE BRANDY CAKE

MABEL OZAKI'S Chocolate Brandy Cake was a prize winner at the Kamuela County Fair, too.

Heat oven to 350, grease and flour two round layer pans, 9x11-1/2 inches.

In large bowl of electric mixer at low speed blend 1 package (18.5 ounces) Devil's Food Cake Mix with 1-1/3 C buttermilk and 2 eggs until moistened. Scrape bowl constantly. Beat 3 minutes on medium speed and keep scraping.

Pour batter in pans and bake until cake springs back when touched lightly in center. . . about 25-30 minutes in 350 oven. Cool in pans about 10 mintues and remove.

Warm 1/3 C honey over low heat, remove and stir in 1/3 C brandy then spoon over bottom of warm cake layers. Cool, then spread Cool Whip between layers and frost generously with same.

Refrigerate until serving time. Additional brandy may be added to the Cool Whip, too.

PUMPKIN PIE

FRANCES DAY'S daughter, MARY WILSON, kindly gave us her mother's recipe for her famous Pumpkin Pies she made for the annual St. Andrew's Bazaar.

Crust: Sift 2 C flour with 1 t salt. Take 1/3 C of the flour and mix with 1/4 C water to form paste. Cut 2/3 C crisco into remaining flour until the size of small peas, stir flour paste into the dough and work by hand until it gathers into a ball. Roll out and place in 10-inch pie tin and use remainder for small pies.

Pumpkin Filling: Mix 1/2 t each ginger, cinnamon, allspice and 1/4 t salt with 1 C sugar, 2 C canned pumpkin, 2 C rich milk and 2 beaten eggs. Pour into unbaked pie crust, bake 15 minutes at 450 and 30 minutes at 350.

MOUNTAIN APPLE PIE

Mountain Apple Pie: Combine 4 C sliced mountain apples, 1/2 t salt, 1 t each cinnamon and nutmeg, 1 C white sugar, 3 T melted butter and juice from 1 lemon. Cook and stir until mountain apples are half done and add 3 T tapioca. Cool.

Pour into unbaked pie shell with either latticed or full crust and bake in 375 oven for about 40-45 minutes.

Suggested eating time. . . while hot!!

MRS. V. P. WOLLASTON has a great pie crust tip. To get a very good bottom pie crust which keeps well, sprinkle bran (the regular health food type) over the lower crust before filling with anything. Especially good with pumpkin. There is no soggy bottom and no one knows it's there. Very good for you, too!

LILIKOI PIE

NANCY VERA CRUZ'S Extra Special Lilikoi Pie melts in the mouth.

Crust: In a bowl combine 1-1/2 C flour, 2 T wheat germ, 2 T chopped walnuts or macadamias, and 3/4 t salt. Cut in 1/2 C shortening (Crisco or 1/2 Crisco and 1/2 oleo). Gradually add 2-3 T water to blend and form ball. Roll out between 2 sheets floured wax paper, place in 9-inch pie plate and bake in 475 oven for 8-10 minutes.

Filling: Sprinkle 1 package unflavored gelatin slowly into 1/4 C water to soak. Cook in double boiler: 1/2 C lilikoi juice, 1/2 t salt, 1/2 C sugar, and 4 egg yolks. Stir constantly until thick, then add the gelatin. Let this cool.

Beat 4 egg whites and slowly add 1/2 C sugar until it holds a peak. Fold into thoroughly cooled lilikoi mixture and pour into baked pie shell. Refrigerate 3-4 hours. To serve add whipped cream!

ICE CREAM PIE

The late LORRAINE COOKE was one of Honolulu's leading hostesses and entertained with a flair. The cooking details were left in the capable hands of her houskeeper and superb French cook, MARGARET COMMUNIEUX. However, Lorraine did have one dish she excelled in for company time.

Lorraine's Ice Cream Pie: Line the bottom of a pie pan with chips of Almond Roca. Then cover with a layer of slightly melted coffee ice cream and freeze. Then add a layer of chocolate ice cream and re-freeze. To serve invert on plate and cut into serving pieces.

FLAN AU CARAMEL

MAGGIE COMMUNEIUX'S Flan Au Caramel may take a little time but well worth it. For the *Caramel:* in a pan over medium temperature put 50 cubes of sugar and 1/4 C water.

As soon as the sugar turns brown put it in 5 oven-proof cups.

For the *Flan:* Bring to a boil 1/2 t vanilla and 2-1/4 C milk, then add 3 beaten eggs and 1/4 C sugar slowly. Pour into cups and place in low pan half filled with water. Cover it with wax paper and bake in 350 oven for half an hour.

HONEY CAKE

KATHRYN MURRY experimented for years to perfect a cake her husband remembered from his childhood. Finally one day he turned to her and said. . . "Why, this is better than my mother's!"

Honey Cake: Cream 6 T softened butter, add 1/2 C sugar gradually, stirring as you add. Fold in 3/4 C honey. Fold in 4 eggs thickly beaten with 1/4 t salt.

Add all at one time: 2 C flour sifted before measuring with 1-1/2 t baking powder, 1/4 t baking soda, and 4 T powdered instant coffee (not freeze-dry).

Keep folding until no flour shows. Fold in grated rind of large navel orange and 1 C walnut pieces, cut not chopped.

Spread evenly on 10x15 inch pan lightly buttered and floured, bake for 35 to 40 minutes or until the cake is medium brown and the edges have separated from the pan. Cool in pan placed on cake rack. When fully cool, cut in squares or bars.

CHEESE CAKE

PRISCILLA GROWNEY'S Pop-In-The-Mouth Cheese Cakes equal 5 or 6 per person, but one very appreciative guest popped 15!

Butter individual mini muffin pans well and press in crumbled graham cracker pie crust, mix and bake.

Fill with your favorite cheese cake mixture and cook accordingly. Let cool, carefully slip a knife around the edges to remove from pan and freeze on cookie sheet.

LEMONADE PIE

BERYL MOIR has a favorite stand-by dessert. . . Lemonade Pie. Bake 2 small graham cracker crusts and cool.

Combine 1 can frozen lemonade, 2/3 can condensed sweetened milk and 1 medium or large (according to tartness) Cool Whip and mix. Pour into crust and freeze.

HAUPIA PUMPKIN PIE

CHARLENE ONO'S Haupia-Pumpkin Pie: Combine 1 pound canned pumpkin and 2 slightly beaten eggs. Stir in 3/4 C sugar, 1/2 t salt and 1 t cinnamon, 1/2 t ginger, 1/4 t cloves. Stir in 1 can evaporated milk and 1 C freshly grated coconut.

Pour into pie shell, bake 15 minutes in 425 oven. Lower heat to 350 and bake for 40 to 45 minutes more or until filling is set. Cool.

Prepare 1 package (2-1/2 ounce) Haupia pudding mix according to instructions and cool slightly. Pour over cooled pie and chill until firm. Just before serving whip 1 C whipping cream and stir in 1 T sugar and spread on pie. Sprinkle with 1/2 C shredded coconut.

GUAVA CAKE

THE WILLOW'S original Guava Cake is world famous. Sift 6 C flour, 4 T baking powder and 1 t salt together. Set aside.

Measure 2 C guava juice and set aside.

Place 1 pound butter and 3 C sugar in mixing bowl and beat until creamy. Add 6 eggs gradually until mixed well with butter mixture. Add flour and juice alternately into butter mixture and mix well but do not over mix. Turn batter into 2 9x12 inch greased pans and bake at 350 for 20 minutes or until done when tested.

GUAVA CHEESE CAKE

ENA SROAT'S Guava Cheese Cake: Beat until smooth one 8-ounce plus 1 3-ounce package of cream cheese (softened), 2 eggs slightly beaten, 1/2 C sugar and 1 t vanilla. Pour into 9-inch graham cracker crust and bake 20 minutes at 350 degrees. Cool.

Topping: Combine 1/2 C sugar, juice of 1/2 lemon, 1-1/2 T cornstarch and 1 can frozen guava juice and cook until thickened. Spread over cheese cake when cooled.

FRUIT CAKE BARS

CHIYONO TAKEMOTO'S Fruit Cake Bars are great for holiday time.

Crust: Cut 2 blocks butter or margarine into 1/2 C confectioner's sugar and 2 C flour. Press into 9x13 inch pan and bake 350 oven for 15 minutes or until brown.

Filling: Sift 1/2 C flour, 1 C sugar, 1/2 t salt and 1 t baking powder and add 4 slightly beaten eggs. Fold in 1 C chopped nuts and 1 C candied fruits. Pour over crust and bake 350 oven for 30 to 40 minutes. Cut when still warm. Sprinkle with powdered sugar.

MANGO MOUSSE

BILL THEOBALD is known as a botanist but his reputation as a cook is gaining renown, too. Try his Mango Mousse and see why! Grind up enough mangoes to make between 4 to 6 C and add, 1 C sugar, juice of 1 lemon, and a jigger of Triple Sec. Mix thoroughly and let stand at room temperature.

Mix 3 envelopes gelatin in 1/2 C cold water, then put over pan of hot water so gelatin dissolves evenly. Pour gelatin mixture into mango mix and stir well. Chill thoroughly.

Whip 3 C heavy cream, chill, and then fold into mango mix. Pour into tubular mold and chill for 1 hour or more. To serve, unmold and fill center with chopped mangoes.

CHOCOLATE MOUSSE

One of MARTHA JUDD'S favorite desserts looks elegant, tastes divine and she confesses that it's the simplest to make. Chocolate Mousse In A Minute: Combine in a blender, 1 6-ounce package semi-sweet chocolate bits, 2 eggs, 2 T rum, cognac or Grand Marnier, 2 to 3 T strong coffee and 3/4 C scalded milk. Whirl at high speed for approximately 2 minutes.

Pour mixture into 6 glass dessert dishes or small ramekins, refrigerate at least 2 hours and serve as is or with dollops of whipped cream on top.

ICE BOX PUDDING

BLANCHE WALKER'S Ice Box Pudding: Line a pan (not tin) with lady fingers (about 2 doz.) Make sauce of 1 T sugar, 6 T ground chocolate, 4 T water, cooked together. While sauce is hot beat in 4 egg yolks plus 2 whites, then fold in 2 egg whites well beaten.

Pour in pan, cover with more lady fingers and stand in ice box over night. Before serving cover with whipped cream.

COCONUT PUDDING

Coconut Pudding: Put 1-1/2 C coconut milk (or plain milk) on stove, add 3 T sugar and 2 T cornstarch and stir well. When it begins to boil, as it thickens add 2 beaten egg whites. When partly cool add 1/2 C grated coconut. Mix well and pour in mould.

CHOCOLATE PUDDING

BLANCHE WALKERS Plain Chocolate Pudding: Beat yolks of 4 eggs and add 1-1/2 C sugar, 10 T grated bread and 5 even T grated chocolate with a little milk from 1 pint. Boil the rest of the pint of milk and pour the mixture into it to thicken, stirring all the time. Add a little vanilla.

Put in pudding dish and bake a few minutes. Beat whites of 4 eggs with 3 T sugar, put on top and brown in oven.

WALNUT CAKE

MRS. H.A. BALDWIN'S Harvard Nut Cakes recipe was written on Halekulani Hotel stationery and dated March sixth, 1922.

Two eggs well beaten, then add in order given 1/2 lb. brown sugar(1 C), 1/2 lb. (1 C) English walnuts, chopped and weighed after being shelled, 3 T flour (or trifle more) which has been sifted with 1/2 t baking powder.

Drop in small t on buttered tins, far enough apart to allow for spreading. Bake in moderate oven.

Tins must be well buttered and very little dropped at a time.

VEGETABLE PUDDING

Another of MRS. BALDWIN'S recipes is written on Moana Hotel stationery and dated Nov. 25, 1921.

English Vegetable Pudding: Mix well 1 C each seeded raisins, currants, grated raw carrots and potatoes and finely chopped suet, 2 C flour mixed with 1-1/2 t (rounded) baking powder, 1 t each cloves, allspice and cinnamon, 1 nutmeg grated and 3 T sugar.

Mix well, and put in well-buttered pudding mould with cover. Set in water which must be boiling. Allow room to increase. Steam 3 hours and serve with Hard Sauce or the following:

Foamy Sauce for Pudding: Beat 2 eggs until light and add 1/2 C granulated sugar and vanilla and add 1 C whipped cream just before serving.

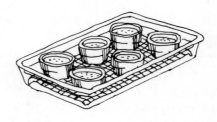

Breads

UN-LEAVENED FUN. . .
BREADS

As I have never been one to mess around with yeast you won't find any such breads here. Maybe in time it will come, but in the meantime here are some of the goodies you can whip up in 'one standing'.

They all freeze well, too, so you can make up several batches with no waiting around.

PINEAPPLE ZUCCHINI BREAD

From San Francisco comes Pineapple Zucchini Bread from MRS. EDITH MOORE. It's delicious and moist. With rotary mixer beat 3 eggs well, add 1 C salad oil, 2 C sugar and 2 t vanilla. Continue beating until thick and foamy. Add and stir up with spoon 2 C coarsely shredded zucchini, 1 8-1/4-ounce can well drained crushed pineapple.

Combine 3 C unsifted flour plus 2 t soda, 1 t salt, 1/2 t baking powder, 2 t ground cinnamon, 1 t ground nutmeg, 1 C each finely chopped macadamia or walnuts and raisins. Stir gently into zucchini mixture until well blended. Divide batter between 2 greased and floured 5x9 loaf pans, bake in 350 oven for 1 hour, cool in pan 10 minutes, turn out on racks to cool thoroughly. . . then partake!

IRISH SODA BREAD

KATHERINE BALDWIN'S Irish Soda Bread is the best! Good for freezing and divine for toast made in oven as you can slice it thick! Combine and mix well: 6 C whole wheat flour, 2 C wheat germ, 2 T sugar, 2 t salt, 2 t baking soda, 1 t baking powder. Add 6 T melted oleo to 1 quart buttermilk and add to dry ingredients. Stir with spoon and knead a few minutes until dough pulls away from sides. Fills two regular loaf tins or several small ones. Bake in 375 oven for 50 minutes or until straw comes out clean.

BRAN MUFFINS

ENA SROAT'S Bran Muffins were an instant hit all around! She says, "One of the greatest and most convenient recipes to come my way in ages. . . bake what you want and refrigerate rest in covered container. Once mixed it keeps indefinitely but *do not* re-mix before using, just dip out and place in well greased muffin tins. And don't use paper muffin liners as they tear off the good sides of the baked muffins. Makes 36 muffins."

Mix first, *cool*, and set aside: 1 C boiling water, 3 C all-bran 100% cereal, 3/4 C white raisins. Cream well: 1-1/2 C sugar, 1/2 C vegetable shortening. Add: 2 eggs, 2-1/2 C flour, 2-1/2 t baking soda, 2 C buttermilk. Combine with first mixture and bake in 400 oven for 20 minutes.

MANGO-MACADAMIA NUT BREAD

CARLA ROBINSON'S Mango-Macadamia Nut Bread was the hit of the church supper! It's rich and moist so needs nothing else. Cream 1/2 C butter with 1 C sugar until frothy, add 2 beaten eggs, puree 1-1/2 C mango with juice of 1/2 lemon or lime and add to mixture blending well. Combine and fold in 2 C flour sifted with 3 t baking powder, 1 t cinnamon, 1 t nutmeg, 1/2 t salt and blend well. Add 1 C chopped macadamia nuts, pour into loaf pan and bake 350 oven for one hour and test with straw to come out clean. Triple the recipe and make 5 7x3x2 aluminum pans to freeze.

BANANA NUT RING OR BREAD

ANITA STUCKY is a great cook and her Banana Nut Ring or Bread is a great innovation —different and freezes well. Beat together 1 3-ounce package cream cheese and 1 C sugar until well blended. Add 1 egg and 1 t vanilla. Stir in 1-1/2 C mashed bananas and 1/2 C chopped pecans. Sift together: 1-1/4 C flour, 3/4 C cornmeal, 1 t each baking powder and soda, 1/2 t each salt, cinnamon, and 1/2 T nutmeg and add to creamed mixture; blend well. Pour into well-greased ring mold or loaf pans. Bake 30-35 minutes at 350 or until toothpick comes out clean. Cool in pan 10 minutes then turn out on rack.

NUT BREAD

Nut Bread: Beat 1 egg slightly. Combine 1/2 C sugar, 1/4 t salt, 1 C graham or whole wheat flour, 1 C white flour, 4 t baking powder and add alternately with 1 C milk to egg. Mix well. Add 1 C chopped macadamia nuts and 1 C chopped raisins. Bake 50 mintues in buttered loaf pan in 350 oven. Gorgeous for buttered tea sandwiches!

COCONUT SHORTBREAD

Coconut Shortbread: Cream 1 C butter with 3 T sugar. Add 2 C sifted flour, 1 C grated coconut, 1 t vanilla. Mix well. Form into 2 rolls as for icebox cookies, wrap in wax paper and thoroughly chill. Slice 1/4 inch thick and bake 30-35 minutes at 300 on ungreased cookie sheet. Remove from pan while warm and sprinkle with sifted powdered sugar. They melt in your mouth!

BREAD

CAPT.(USN RET) FRANK FULLAWAY introduced me to this fabulous Bread recipe and the self rising flour opened whole new doors! Simple, simple, simple!!

Mix 3 C *Self-Rising Flour* with 3 T sugar and add 1 can beer! No need to knead, no need to let rise, just mix well, have the last sip of beer, put in bread loaf pan, bake 350 oven for 1 hour or until brown and crusty and dry when toothpick inserted. Gorgeous toast with a 'come here' aroma!

Bring the can of beer to room temperature before making the bread.

BANANA BREAD

In a hurry? Have a bumper crop of bananas? Puree bananas in blender and freeze by cupfulls and make banana bread later. Using the boxed ready-mixed yellow cake mix: follow the directions and substitute banana puree for the liquid plus the eggs. Quick, simple and good. You might want to coarsely chop some banana and add to it, too, for texture.

MANGO BREAD

HARUYO KIMURA'S Mango Bread is really moist and keeps well.

Beat 6 eggs, add 2 C oil, 4 C flour, 3 C sugar, 4 t soda, 1 t salt, 4 t cinnamon, 2 t vanilla, 1/2 C chopped macadamia or walnuts, 1 C grated coconut and 4 C mashed or chopped ripe mangoes (Haden preferably).

Beat in electric mixer until well blended. Bake at 350 for 1 hour in five greased and floured bread loaf pans.

GINGER BREAD

ELOISE WINSTEDT found this recipe for Ginger Bread in her mother's old recipe book and says it is a particularly delicious version and the tea makes all the difference.

Cream 1/2 C brown sugar with 1/2 C butter, add 1 slightly beaten egg and 1/2 C light molasses. Cream until fluffy.

Sift together and add 1-1/2 C sifted flour, 1/4 t salt, 1 t each cinnamon and ginger, and 1/2 t powdered cloves.

Add 1 t baking soda dissolved in 1/2 C hot tea. Pour mixture into buttered loaf pan and bake 25 to 30 minutes in 350 oven until tester comes out clean.

PEANUT BUTTER BREAD

JOANNE RUSSELL'S Peanut Butter Bread is a variation of her basic recipe that she switches around at will.

With hand mixer, cream 1/2 C shortening with 1 C sugar and 2 eggs until fluffy and smooth.

Beat in 1/2 C crunchy (or plain) peanut butter mixed with a drop or 2 of water.

Combine 2 C flour with 2 t baking soda and slowly add this to the first mixture. Pour into well greased loaf pan and bake in 350 oven for 40 to 50 minutes. When you take the cake out of the oven, poke a few holes in the top and dribble over the following topping: 1/2 C

peanut butter mixed with enouth water to thin. Instead of water Joanne sometimes uses mashed bananas.

The variations are many. . . instead of adding the peanut butter, add 1/2 C apple sauce and 1 C raisins; or use 3 eggs and add 1 C chopped dates and 1 C of nuts. Or add 1 C fruit cake mix (chopped), 1 T grated orange rind, and 1 C nuts.

If you use the basic recipe with 2 eggs for wet additions and 3 eggs for dry, you can try all sorts of combinations.

SHORTBREAD SQUARES'

AMY SAKIHAMA says these Shortbread Squares are so delicious, so firm and substantial that she usually doubles the recipe in a 9x12 inch pan.

Beat 2 blocks of butter with 1/2 C sugar well with mixer. Add 2-1/3 C flour mixed with 1/4 t salt. Mix well.

Grease 8x8 inch pan. Press batter into pan, using wax paper so your hands don't get messy. Prick with fork. Place in 300 oven about 1-1/2 hours. Cut into squares when slightly cool.

Optional: place in refrig about 1/2 hour before baking.

MANGO SHORTBREAD

When CRYSTAL KANNA brought me her mother's 'add-a-pound', it was made from Bartlett pears from their own garden. So you can use a variety of fruit. It's Delicious Mango Shortbread. Cream 1-1/2 C butter with 1 C sugar. Add 3 C sifted flour. Press half of this mixture into greased 9x13 inch pan.

Mix: 4 C sliced mangoes, 1/2 C sugar (less according to sweetness of fruit), 1/4 C flour, 1-1/2 t cinnamon and dash of nutmeg if desired. Pour mixture over dough. Crumble other half of dough over fruit mixture. Bake 1 hour in 350 oven.

CRANBERRY COFFEE CAKE

DIANA SCHUMAN makes this Cranberry Coffee Cake in nothing flat. . . a little something she picked up by scanning the recipes on boxes.

Mix 1/4 C brown sugar, 1/2 C chopped walnuts, 1/4 t cinnamon and set aside.

Combine 2 C biscuit mix, 2 T sugar, 1 egg, 2/3 C water or milk, and beat vigorously 1/2 minute.

Spread batter in greased square pan. . . 9x9x2 inches. . . and sprinkle with the nut mixture. Spoon 2/3 C whole cranberry sauce over the top. Bake 20 to 30 minutes in 350 oven. Serves 9.

STRAWBERRY NUT BREAD

JUANITA MAMACLAY'S Strawberry Nut Bread: Cream together 1 block butter or oleo, 3/4 C granulated sugar, 1/2 t vanilla, and 1/2 t lemon extract until light and fluffy. Add 2 extra large eggs, one at a time, beating well after each addition.

Sift together 1-1/2 C flour, 1/2 t each salt and cream of tartar, and 1/4 t soda.

Combine 2/3 C strawberry preserves and 1/4 C strawberry yogurt. Add yogurt mixture to creamed mixture alternately with dry ingredients. Stir in 1/2 C chopped walnuts.

Pour batter into greased 9x5 inch pan,

bake in 350 oven for about 1 hour or until toothpick comes out clean. Cool for 10 minutes, remove from pan, cool completely, wrap in foil, and refrigerate for 24 hours before slicing. Freezes nicely, too.

BEER BISCUITS

Beer Biscuits: Combine 2 C bisquick with 3 T sugar and add 3/4 C of *warm beer*. Drop the batter from a tablespoon into well greased muffin tins, bake at 400 for 20 minutes. They puff up like popovers but have an irregular, crusty, browned surface. Makes 12 fantastic biscuits!

MANGO BREAD

The late PHOEBE FITZGERALD'S Mango Bread tends to be more moist as she used cut-up ripe mangoes instead of the pureed. Cream 1 C shortening and 3/4 C sugar, and add 3 eggs.

Sift 3 C flour with 1 t soda, 1-1/2 t baking powder and 1/2 t salt.

Sprinkle 2 T lime juice over 2 C or little more of cut-up ripe mango. Add flour mixture and mango alternately to creamed mixture. Mix well and add 1/2 C chopped nuts. Bake in 2 greased medium size loaf pans in 375 oven for about 1 hour.

QUICK WHOLE WHEAT BREAD

FRAN BROSSY'S Quick Whole Wheat Bread for those of you on schedules.

Beat 1/4 C sugar and 1 egg together. Beat in 1/2 C molasses and 1 T vegetable oil or margarine. Then add 1 C whole wheat flour, 2/3

C all purpose flour, 1 C buttermilk, 1 t baking soda and 1/2 t salt.

Put in greased and floured 9x5x3 inch loaf pan and let stand 15 minutes. Bake in 350 oven for 40 minutes. Cool before cutting.

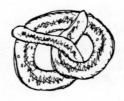

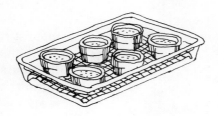

Gifts

**FROM MY KITCHEN TO YOUR HOUSE
WITH LOVE
HOME MADE GOODIES**

You really don't need an occassion or an excuse to take a friend some goodies! Sharing it's called. To be sure the days seem to be so full, but it's good every once in a while to take time out and create a 'goodie' in your kitchen with some to spare and share. Take it to a friend and have a lovely visit.

LAVASH

What do you give someone who has everything? Home-made Lavash. Conserve your strength for this one, tho, it takes a lot of action with the rolling pin!

Mix 2-3/4 C flour, 1/4 C sugar, 1/2 t salt, 1/2 t baking soda, 1 T each sesame and poppy seeds. Cut in 1 block of butter. Mix in 1 C buttermilk.

When well mixed, positively, smear a large surface with flour and you may either roll out teaspoonfulls of dough at a time or larger quantities, whichever. . . but be sure and roll it out as thin as possible! Keep pouring on the flour and turning to roll evenly. Bake on ungreased cookie sheet, til brown, about 12 minutes in 350 to 375 degree oven. An extra pair of hands to spoon and roll is a great help!

GUAVA RELISH

You can use Guava Relish instead of tomato for many things, and especially good over a block of cream cheese to serve with crackers.

Cut half ripe and a few green guavas in half, remove every trace of seed (use this for puree later) then slice and chop very small. Combine 2 C guava with 2 C each finely chopped cabbage, green and red bell peppers, round onions, and a liberal helping of chopped garlic and as many chopped Hawaiian Chili peppers as you dare!

In a pot bring to a boil little less than a quart of vinegar and 2 C brown sugar, 2 T Hawaiian salt, 1 t each powdered cloves, celery seed, allspice and tumeric then add the chopped guava and veggies. Let this simmer down for about 2 hours to a thick consistency and bottle as usual. Try to find red bell peppers as it does add such a pretty color to the jar. . . especially for Christmas giving. Tomato relish can be made the same way when they're falling off the vine.

COCONUT CANDY

HAZEL KAUAHIKAUA'S Coconut Candy recipe is one which she has used for many years to send to the mainland. Bring to a good rolling boil: 3 C sugar, and 3/4 C fresh milk. Add 3 C grated fresh coconut, pinch of salt and 1 t white distilled vinegar. Cook until soft ball stage. Remove from fire, add 1 t vanilla and beat until ready to drop on waxed paper by teasponfuls.

GINGER PEACHES

HARRIET WARREN'S Ginger Peaches are a raging success with any entree! Drain a 29-ounce can peach halves. Combine 3/4 C syrup with 1/2 C cider vinegar, add 1 C light brown sugar and 1 t ground ginger. Simmer 5 minutes. Add peaches. Simmer 5 minutes longer. Chill and serve. A few apricots may be added for color.

MELON AND GINGER JAM

How many of you remember the delicious IXL brand of preserves we bought years ago? Think it came from Argentina. If you want to duplicate the Melon and Ginger Jam for yourself and holiday giving, MAY MOIR'S recipe is tops.

Three pounds Chinese melon (also called white melon; Deng-Kwa in Chinese; and Togwa in Japanese. The Latin name is Benincasacerifera). Cut melon into very small dices, 1/4 inch or less, add 1/2 C water and simmer for an hour, stirring at first. As the melon simmers add 1 thumb finely chopped ginger. Measure the melon and add an equal amount of sugar. Stir in the juice of one lemon. Thinly slice half of another lemon and add the slices, rind and all. Boil all together until the jam jells. Better jar in large-size sterilized jars!

RICE CRISPIES CANDY

ANITA STUCKY makes an easy version of Rice Crispies Candy: Bring to just boiling point 1 C white sugar, 1 C white karo, remove from heat and blend in 1 C peanut butter. Fold in 6 C rice crispies. Press in 13x8 buttered pan. Cut into squares when cool.

RUM DUM BALLS

Fill jars with Rum Dum Balls! Mix all together: 3 C ground vanilla wafer crumbs, 1 C chopped macadamia nuts, 1 C powdered sugar, 1/8 t salt, 3 T light corn syrup, and 1/2 to 3/4 C Rum. Mix, mash, knead all together and form into bite-size balls, roll in lots of powdered sugar and the longer they mellow the better. . . in air tight jars!

HOT MUSTARD

"The best part of any ham," says BARBARA BRYAN "is the Hot Mustard you make at home." Blend well and cook over low heat stirring constantly. . . 1/3 C sugar, 1/3 C Coleman's mustard, 1/3 C vinegar and one slightly beaten egg. Continue cooking until mixture thickens and bubbles. Keep refrigerated.

CRANBERRY SAUCE

Want to make your own Cranberry Sauce? Boil together for 5 minutes: 1 C water and 2 C sugar. Add 1 pound rinsed and drained cranberries and cook 5 minutes or until all have popped and become transparent. Remove from fire and add 6 generous T orange marmalade. Stir. Add strained juice from 2 lemons. Bottle and refrigerate.

SHERRY CRANBERRY

Sherry Cranberry is different. Dissolve 1 C granulated sugar in 1 C dry sherry over low heat stirring continually. Add 2 C pierced cranberries and 1/2 C coarsely ground walnuts and simmer until cranberries are thoroughly cooked but not mushy. Try it cold, plain, or over lemon sherbert or ice cream; hot over apple pie! Mmm! Jar and refrigerate.

GRANOLA

Granola is always a welcome gift. Combine 6 C quick old fashioned oats, 1/2 C firmly packed brown sugar, 1/2 C wheat germ, 1/2 C shredded coconut, 1/2 C sesame seed, 1 C chopped nuts and stir in 1/2 C vegetable oil, 1/2 C honey and 2 t vanilla. Bake in ungreased pan in 300 oven for 20-30 minutes stirring often to brown evenly. Stir until crumbly. Store in tightly covered containers.

INAMONA

Inamona was a simple but essential condiment made from the nuts of *Kukui* trees. You can either buy it in the markets or make it yourself. It's easy. Roast the whole *kukui* nut slowly in oven for at least 1/2 hour until brown, crack open and remove kernel of meat. Pound with rock or blunt end of knife. . . don't chop. . . add a pinch of Hawaiian salt and fry for a few minutes then bottle. If you're fixing to polish your calabashes with the meat wrapped in piece of cloth, don't bother to fry it, just bag and rub!

BRANDIED FRUIT

This Brandied Fruit recipe for a starter caused quite a rumble and VIRGINIA WELSH's version is called *"Friendship Cup"*. Start with 1 C pineapple chunks, drained, 1 C sugar and let stand 2 weeks in warm place. Then add 1 C sliced peaches, drained and 1 C sugar. Let stand 2 weeks, then add: 1 C maraschino cheries, drained and 1 C sugar.

Let stand 2 weeks then repeat entire procedure transferring to larger container as needed. Never refrigerate. Not at any time let this amount fall below 1-1/2 C or it will not work. Delicious over vanilla ice cream. When you give a starter to a friend, remember to keep a cup and a half for yourself and then half fill small containers that have loose fitting tops and instructions for carrying on the process. Use only glass and wooden utensils!

BREAD AND BUTTER PICKLES

Once you give away these Bread and Butter Pickles you'll be beseiged for the recipe! Slice 6 quarts cucumbers, 12 medium onions, 4 large green bell peppers and soak with 1 C Hawaiian salt for 3 hours. Wash. Heat in large kettle: 1/4 C mustard seed, 2 T celery seed, 2 t tumeric, 10 C sugar, 2-1/2 quarts vinegar. Bring to the boiling point and throw in cukes etc. Seal in sterilized jars. Let them stand a week or more before you give away.

MANGO CHUTNEY I

Special Mango Chutney is a sure winner and will endear you to *malihini* and *kamaaina* alike! Soak 50 common mangoes, about 8-9 pounds of slices with generous sprinkling of Hawaiian salt for three hours. Boil together 5 pounds sugar and 1 quart vinegar until syrupy. Drain and slightly rinse half of sliced mangoes and add to syrup. Cook about 20-30 minutes and add the rest of the drained mangoes and the following ingredients: 1 pound currants, 1 pound seeded raisins, 1/2 pound blanched almonds (optional), jar preserved ginger chopped and the juice, 1/2 C citron chopped, 1/2 C fresh ginger grated or chopped or sliced, 3 large onions chopped, 3 cloves garlic (or more) finely chopped, 1 package lemon peel sliced, 1 package orange peel, chopped or sliced. You may want to put these all through the meat grinder. According to your taste buds either add 3-6 de-seeded and finely sliced red Hawaiian chili peppers or put them in a bag to cook and remove when done.

To all this add: 4 T salt, 1 t each ginger, cinnamon, allspice. Cook until mangoes are quite brown and done. . . about 1-3 hours, stirring frequently. Jar immediately.

Through the years I have chucked the package peels and substituted 2 cartons of mixed glazed fruits. Canned apricots are good, too. The addition of sliced whole lemons, oranges and even grapefruit gives it a new twist. For a real taste change try adding a few anise stars. Chutney seems to getting scarcer and scarcer so if you can find the mangoes stock up!

MANGO CHUTNEY II

Spur of the Moment Mango Chutney is simple and not all that time-consuming. Peel and slice 25 large half-ripe mangoes into large pot. . . about 5 C. Add 1-1/2 C vinegar, 2 C sugar, shakes of allspice, cinnamon, cloves, nutmeg, ginger, a few big pinches of Hawaiian salt and then raid the larder.

Chop up 4 large onions, lots of garlic (more the merrier), grate and slice a large finger of ginger, de-seed and chop up 3 red hot chili peppers (or douse to taste with tabasco), slice and sliver a whole lemon, orange and grapefruit and also some Chinese salty lemon peel. Toss any or all into the pot and let bubble along for about 3 hours. Net result 12 small jars of the best chutney!

KIM CHEE

Kim Chee: Cut up any cabbage, (preferably won bok), *daikon*, cucumbers or mix all together. Sprinkle with Hawaiian salt until well soaked. . . about 2-3 hours. Put veggies in quart bottle and add 2 T packaged Kim Chee mix, 1 C water, sliced garlic and dash of aji. Let stand at least 2 days before indulging.

DRIED SLICED MANGOES

IRENE NOZAKI shares one way to use up the bumper mango crop with this delicious Dried Sliced Mangoes. Slice mangoes 1/4 inch thick, fill baking pan 3/4 full and put as many as your oven will hold at 300 degrees. Turn every 15 minutes and drain off liquid or use the baster. Keep removing the liquid for at least 1-1/2 to 2 hours.

However, if you have to go shopping just turn off the oven and continue process when you return. When all the liquid is gone, you can dry the slices outside in the sun for 2-3 days or place the slices on cookie sheet and dry off in warm oven until really dried.

If you don't have a fish box to lay the slices in, lay the mangoes on foil-covered cookie sheet and cover with thin gauze so no bugs can get in, and dry in sun. Either way, keep turning during this last process. Irene has found that they retain the lovely orange color while drying in the oven but blacken in the box. However, they're still tasty!

DILL PICKLES

VELMA LUMMIS has a neat trick she does to spruce up a simple ole jar of dill pickles. Buy the large jar of Dill Pickles, drain all the liquid off, add 1 C of sugar and 1 t dried red peppers. Put jar in refrigerator and shake every few days. It will make its own juice and in three weeks. . . if they last that long. . they will be sweet *hot* pickles!

PRESERVED KUMQUATS

MARGARET ZABRISKIE puts a new twist into Preserved Kumquats. Wash and de-stem 6 C kumquats, steep in boiling water for 2 minutes, drain, cook gently in boiling water for 20 minutes, drain; make syrup by boiling 3 C water with 3 C sugar plus about 1 t grated ginger root.

Drain the kumquats and add to this syrup and simmer gently for about 20 minutes or until they appear glossy. Don't cook them fast or they'll pop and shrivel. When cooked pour into sterilized jars leaving room for 1 ounce brandy per 1/2 pint jar, or proportionately.

FIG MUI

ELAINE LINDSEY thought she was buying a bargain on prunes only to discover once she got home that she'd grabbed figs instead. So she simply made Fig Mui instead.

Mix all together in large bowl: 8 (1 pound) packages figs (or prunes), 1-1/2 C pure lemon juice, 1 t Five Spices, 1 large package each dried lemon peel and seedless *li-hing mui*, 1 pound brown sugar and 1 T Hawaiian salt.

Mix thoroughly and put in gallon jar. Let this stand on kitchen table so you can turn it upside down several times a day for at least a week. . . or as many days as you or the kiddies can wait!

SAUCE FOR HAM

SARAH WILDER'S Home-made Sauce for Ham: Melt 2 T each butter and currant jelly, add 2 T sherry, 1 T each Worcestershire, tarragon vinegar and 1/2 t dry mustard. Combine and beat well. Jar and keep refrigerated.

GUAVA JELLY TIPS

Remember to pick both half-ripe and

green guavas along with the ripe, too, so the pectin content will be high.

Add a dab of butter to the cooking jelly so it won't scum.

The jelly is done when 2 or 3 drops run together and sheet to form one big blob off the spoon.

If guava jelly doesn't jell. . . store it separately and use to mix with ice cream, dribble over baked or fried bananas, or for pancakes! Don't fret, it happens to the experts too. . . and there are varieties of guavas that never do jell!

BASIC GUAVA JELLY

Basic Guava Jelly: Simmer chopped guavas in large pot and add just enough water to come just below the top of the fruit. Cook until mushy and well done.

Pour into special bags made of netting or regular strainers and let drip for liquid. The bags make a clearer liquid for jelly. Save the pulp for jam.

Measure cup of juice for C of sugar and do not cook more than 3 C at a time. Bring to a good rolling boil but watch it so it doesn't overflow. Add the dab of butter, keep at rolling boil, and skim off whatever scum appears. The shorter the cooking, the quicker the evaporation and clearer the jelly.

Jar when it sheets off the spoon.

Put the guava pulp through a sieve or food mill for puree to make jam.

If you like tart jam, combine 1 C puree with 3/4 C sugar and add a splash of lemon juice. Otherwise combine 1 C pulp and 1 C sugar.

The optional additions are: lemon juice,

dash of cinnamon, nutmeg, cloves, grated or powdered ginger and allspice.

Bring the mixture to a boil, turn down to low, cover the pot and let it cook slowly so it doesn't burn the bottom of the pot. Stir frequently and it is ready when it thickens and sheets from the spoon.

CRANBERRY CHUTNEY

MILDRED MEAD'S Cranberry Chutney is a great gift item. In a large deep saucepan combine 4 C whole cranberries (fresh or frozen) with 2-1/2 C sugar, 1 C water, 6 whole cloves, 2 cinnamon sticks and 1/2 t salt. Bring to boil, stirring frequently. Cook 10 minutes or until berries pop. Add 1 C light raisins, 2 tart apples and pears peeled, cored and diced, 1 small onion chopped, and 1/2 C sliced celery.

Continue stirring and cooking until thick, about 15 minutes. Remove from heat and sitr in 1/2 C chopped walnuts and 1 t lemon zest. Ladle into sterilized jars and process in boiling water for 10 minutes. (2 quarts.)

If you like it hot, add some minced or grated ginger to taste.

HAWAIIAN CHILI PEPPERS

GLADYS BORRERO taught me how to use all the little red Hawaiian chili peppers that were blooming like mad. . . and also save on buying store-bought *hot sauce!*

Pick enough red chili peppers to fill a pint jar 3/4 full. The stems must be removed so it's best to use plastic gloves, and pick and jar right from the bush.

Add 2 T Hawaiian salt and cover with vinegar to the top. Leave in refrigerator for 4 to 5 days and check in a day to see that vinegar is still on top. Empty jar into blender and let it whirl. Strain over several layers of cheese cloth into wide mouth jar and funnel the gorgeous colored liquid into an old Worcestershire bottle.

Be sure and clean the blender thoroughly afterwards!!

SWEET DILL PICKLES

MILDRED MEAD said these Sweet Dill Pickles were so good it's unbeliveable, and how right she was! So crisp they bite you! Halve or quarter whole dill pickles and drain. Heat to boiling 1 C cider vinegar, 2 C sugar and 2 T pickling spices. Pour over pickles, cool and refrigerate. Next morning, pour off the liquid and bring to a boil again, pour back over the pickles, cool and refrigerate. They're ready for crunching in a couple of days.

LILIKOI JELLY

NATSUKO TERAMOTO'S Lilikoi Jelly is the best ever and her method retains the fruit's special flavor. Bring 3 C sugar and 1 C water to a boil and boil hard for 1 minute. Remove from stove and add 1 bag of Certo and mix well. Add 1/2 C *lilikoi* juice, skim and pour jelly into sterilized jars.

....Extras....

MISCELLANEOUS

PANCAKES

DAVID EYRE'S Pancakes recipe was first printed in the Sunday New York Times in full color in the rotogravure section. When Craig Claiborne was asked to name the most popular recipe ever printed in the food columns of the New York Times, without missing a breath he named David's pancakes! And he's so right!

In a mixing bowl, combine 1/2 C flour, 1/2 C milk, 2 eggs lightly beaten, pinch of nutmeg. Beat lightly, leaving the batter a little lumpy. Melt 4 T butter in a 12-inch skillet with heatproof handle (glass baking dish works fine, too).

Pour in batter and bake in 425 oven 15-20 minutes or until pancake is golden brown. Sprinkle 2 T confectioners' sugar and juice of half a lemon over and return briefly to oven. Serve with jelly, jam or marmalade. Yeild 2-4 servings.

David adds: "Leave out the nutmeg, lemon and powdered sugar and have a fine 'shell' for creamed chicken. Use as dessert pancakes and add peaches, strawberries or other fruits at the very last moment. Or slosh the basic pancake with Cointreau, Tripple Sec, dark rum or whatever you find in the liquor cabinet. You might also want to add more nutmeg, powdered sugar, and lemon juice after you've experimented a few times."

SEASONED FLOUR

Seasoned Flour: Mix in blender until powdery: 1/3 package Shake 'n Bake, 2 C flour, 1 C oatmeal and add to 1 C bread crumbs, 3-4 T garlic powder, 1/2 C wheat germ and salt and pepper. Stir and blend well and keep available in cannister or jar.

SALT DUCK EGGS

Salt Duck Eggs: Salt solution: 1-1/2 C salt to gallon of water. Boil and cool when salt is dissolved. Drop in raw duck or chicken eggs and let stand submerged for a month..

To serve: boil egg 20 minutes, peel and

halve. The longer they're in the jar the saltier the egg, but if they're to your taste, remove and refrigerate.

SALTED MUSTARD CABBAGE

Salted Mustard Cabbage; Use same salt solution as in salt eggs and cool. Clean whole head mustard cabbage, dip in boiling water slightly, cool, place in salt brine for 3 to 5 days. Either slice and eat plain or cook (stir fry) with sliced pork or beef.

BOVRIL BUTTER

Bovril Butter is another handy jar to have on hand. Mix even parts of Bovril and butter, sprinkle in ample amount of parmesan cheese and blend well. Keeps a good while, too.

HERB BUTTER

Herb Butter is handy to have sitting in the refrig. Cream 1/3 pound sweet butter and add freshly, finely chopped T parsely, chives, and sweet basil. To serve, spread generously on both sides of sliced French bread before warming, on toasted rounds or you can even add this to scrambled eggs, too.

TIPS

Instead of the usual pinch of sugar when using tomatoes in stews or soups, try popping in a few raisins or prunes. Nummy and nutritous.

Want to make your own herb boquets? Combine a pinch to 1/2 t each of herbs desired, tie mixture in cheesecloth to facilitate removal and add to soups, etc.

Beef: marjoram, savory, basil, thyme, parsley, oregano.

Eggs and Chicken: tarragon, basil, chives and savory.

Vegetables: basil, savory, chives and marjoram.

Soups and Stews: parsley, thyme, basil, marjoram, rosemary and savory.

To make a nifty gift item for your next bazaar why not wrap different 'flavors' with various colored rick-rack, place 4 of each in the likes of an old candy box and paste the info on the lid!

To polish those prized calabashes: bake *kukui* nuts in 350 oven 30 minutes. Crack and remove the kernels from the nut, chop slightly and tie securely in a durable square of material.

Then rub, rub, rub and rub some more inside and our of your heirlooms. They are probably so dry and thristy you'll only have the patience and energy to do one at a time. . . but, oh, so worth it!

MRS MANA VENABLE suggests using a piece of *ti* leaf just the size or a fraction larger than the food to be steamed in collapsible steamer or bowl. At serving time leaf and all can be lifted to plate. Super for fish fillets or reviving cold rice. . . and it also adds flavor.

To stuff the halved whites of hard boiled eggs, mash the yolks according to your favorite recipe then spoon mixture into the tube of a cake icer. Pick your decorator nozzle and push down on the plunger. The whites are so easy to fill and there is no mess on the edges.

And if you want to be fancy, garnish with small bits of parsley, bits of green or ripe olives, red cavier and on and on!

Out of oranges and lemons to complete your old-fashioned cocktail? Fret not, just put in a dollop of marmalade and leave off the sugar.

HORSERADISH MOUSSE

Another goodie from the Academy of Arts Garden Cafe menu. . . Horseradish Mousse. Serve it as a garnish for roast beef sandwiches.

Whip 1/2 C whipping cream and gently fold in: 3 T well-drained prepared horseradish, 1/4 t salt, 2 t grated onion and 1 t lemon juice. Chill.

SWISS CHEESE CROQUETTES

Swiss Cheese Croquettes: Make a very thick white sauce and stir in 1/2 t hot mustard, 1 T finely cut green pepper, and cool to room temperature.

Fold in 1 C finely diced Swiss cheese. Now measure out 1/3 C portions and roll in 1/2 C fine dry bread crumbs. Chill thoroughly.

Roll again in more crumbs, then in mixture of 1 beaten egg and 1 T water, and back to the crumbs again. Place in refrigerator to firm up.

Fry them in 365 degree skillet with ample shortening until golden brown. You have to keep turning these to brown evenly. Lift out, drain on paper towels and serve hot.

MACARONI AND CHEESE CASSEROLE

From Lahaina, Maui, LEATHA GILLIS has gloriously shattered the archaic method of making Macaroni and Cheese Casserole. This beautiful one-step-only favorite alleviates cleaning messy old pots, too.

Leatha writes. . . "Boil your mac, then pour as much of the water off as possible when it is just beginning to be al dente. Simply put the butter in mac pan and stir thoroughly. Shake or sift flour into pan and stir well. Add milk and when it begins to thicken, the cheese may be added in smallish chunks and will melt nicely.

"Or if you prefer the marbling method. . . fold in strips of cheese the last minute. Leave in double boiler to wait dinner while you toss the green salad.

"If you like serving it in a casserole, you can sprinkle grated cheese on top and brown it under the broiler a minute or two."

YORKSHIRE PUDDING

NETTY HANSEN has a super recipe for Yorkshire Pudding. In a large bowl combine 1-1/2 C sifted flour with 1 T each nutmeg, salt and pepper. Make a well and gradually add 4 well beaten eggs combined with 1-1/2 C milk. Stir well and beat several minutes.

Cover with cloth and chill in refrig about 2 hours.

When your roast is done and out of the oven, put 1/2 C drippings in shallow pan, (fat should be 1/2 inch deep), place in oven until sizzling hot. Pour in chilled batter which has been beaten again for several minutes to form

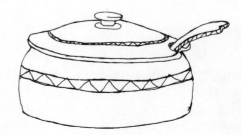

bubbles. Bake 15 minutes at 450 or until pudding has risen.

Reduce heat to 300 and bake another 15 minutes until pudding is brown and crisp. Cut in squares and place around your beautiful roast. Eat immediately and enjoy.

AMAZING PIE

When is a pie not a pie? You'll have to try this Amazing Pie several times several ways to believe it!

Into blender put 1/2 C Bisquick, 1/2 C sugar, 4 eggs, 2 C milk, 1 C grated carrots, 3 T butter, and chopped green or white onions, optional.

Turn mixer to blend and mix thoroughly. Pour into 9 inch buttered pie pan. Bake in 400 oven first 10 minutes, 350 for 20 minutes or until custard sets and knife comes out clean.

Let it cool and serve as vegetable with steak or roast.

Would you believe the crust is on the bottom? Or course it has been known to be on top, but then you just slice a piece and turn it upside down on the plate. . . who's to know!

You can leave out the carrots and onions and add 1 t vanilla and have plain custard pie, or add 1 C coconut or bananas, even zucchini, or just use your own imagination.

CREAM PUFFS

CHRIS, the chef at Kapiolani Hospital brightens the ladies' day with these home-made goodies.

Cream Puffs: melt 1/2 pound butter in 2 C boiling water. Add and beat vigorously 2 C sifted flour and 1/2 t salt, remove from fire as soon as mixture leaves the sides of the pan. Cool in mixing bowl, add 8 eggs, one at a time beating after each addition. (a cuisinart is great for this.) Measure with Number 24 dipper and drop on oiled sheet pan. Bake 45 minutes at 375.

Filling: Dilute 1 C cornstarch with water, add 4 eggs and 4 C sugar. Stir into 2 quarts hot milk, cook one minute or until thick. Slit puffs, fill, dust with powdered sugar.

You may fill these with ice cream at the last moment, too, but at home only. For the hospital Cris tops these cream puffs with chocolate sauce.

You can use the same batter and drop by t and bake for pupu puffs. These freeze well and can be filled with a variety of fillings. . . chicken, tuna, ham, egg, and olive mixes, and many more.

MACADAMIA NUT SAUCE

MAX T. MORI, the famous chef at Kona Inn years ago created 3 great sauces.

Macadamia Nut Sauce A La Kona Inn: Melt 1/2 pound butter, 1 T lemon juice, 1/4 C white wine (Sauterne), and 1/4 C broken bits of macadamia nuts. Let mixture simmer over low heat 15 minutes and add 1 t ajinomoto.

FRESH ROOT GINGER SAUCE

Fresh Root Ginger Sauce: This recipe makes 1 quart and is excellent for baked desserts.

Melt 1/2 pound butter, add 1 small finely chopped ginger root and cook 5 minutes. Add 1/4 C flour, 1/2 C brown sugar and dash of salt. Cook about 3 minutes and gradually add 1 C coconut honey and 1 quart heavy cream. Continue cooking until smooth, stirring all the time. Remove from heat, strain, cool, and if too thick, adjust consistency by adding heavy cream to desired texture. Keep refrigerated.

KONA COFFEE SAUCE

Kona Coffee Sauce: Melt 4 ounces butter, add 1/2 C brown sugar, 1 ounce soluble Sanka coffee, 2 T flour and cook until well blended. Gradually add mixture of 1/4 C condensed milk, 1 C black coffee, and 3/4 C coconut honey. Cook until mixture is smooth. Remove from fire, cool, and fold into 1 C whipped cream. (1 C crushed pineapple optional.)

SURVIVAL KIT

MARTHA JUDD'S 'survival kit' has saved many a picnic, and you could make one too! Strung on stout braided twine are the essentials: folding scissors, spreading knife, paring knife with a cork at the tip end for protection, a can opener that turns, combination bottle opener-cork screw in a plastic container, 'do-it-all' scissors, tiny pruning cutters, and a midget-king knife.

RAY LAUCHIS says: "I love to cook and put a lot of myself into my cooking. Yesterday I grated in some of my thumb."

....Entertaining....

SO YOU WANT TO GIVE A PARTY!

Beginning to feel uneasy going to parties lately? Find yourself hedging around potted plants and averting your eyes when Mrs. "What's with you" enters a crowded room? Did you read a hidden meaning into Mary's remark about 'having people over for dinner'? People beginning to look at you as tho you're half-starved and on relief? You're really dead at the bank when Mrs. "Well I'll tell You'!" corners you with. . . "Say, don't you ever entertain?"

You can think of a hundred excuses. . . all valid, maybe. . . but the fact remains that if you accept someone else's bread and butter, wine and cheese, pheasant and champagne. . . *whatever. . . you are going to have a party!* The alternative? Continue chatting with the butcher, laundryman, the lady next door while hanging clothes. . . all very cozy, too, and doesn't cost a penny or involve a sip or a bite!

Fortunately, here in Hawaii entertaining is more informal and the likes of cocktail parties or buffets are among the most popular. However, you just don't bingo have a party!!

Oh, no! It takes thought, time and *planning!* Unless, of course, you have a vast staff below in the domestic department.

Over the years a *check list* has proven the biggest asset to entertaining! Grab yourself a handy notebook and you'll be off and away!

Set the date. Mid week is best except for a Friday or Saturday gala-gala when you don't mind sitting up with 'those precious few' to watch the sun rise from your *lanai* and you can sleep until Monday.

Will it be a special occasion? Cocktails? Brunch? Picnic? Buffet Supper? or Seated Dinner? Decide and then. . .

Make out your guest list. Keep within a number you, your husband, your home and hopefully hired help can manage nicely. Try to gather a congenial group. . . maybe with just a sprinkling of a few of the odd "I-O-U's". For heaven's sake forget 'fun and games' and home-brewed movies or worse yet slides with running commentary! Taint no time to trap your guests!

Decide on your menu. . . according to the occasion and keeping your check book very much in mind! Once you've set the date, etc.

watch the market ads for specials. It can influence your whole menu. Turkeys on special? Grab one, cook it up for the family then cream a scrumptious casserole, make dainty sandwiches, or leave cold for buffet make-your-own sandwiches for the party.

Engage extra help if necessary or possible. So worth it, expecially after the Ball is over. Your husband would rather forego a round of drinks and golf rather than be caught dead over the sink at midnight.

Don't ever trust your memory! Write it all down. Plan, plan, plan. Make lists and don't go off and leave the lists on the piano like my old friend who used to say, "Shoogleberries, should have brought the piano!"

Use a big sheet of paper and make up your own menu:

Dish: Potato chips and clam dip.

On hand: 2 cans minced clams

To buy: Cream cheese

From freezer: Maui potato chips

Check liquor supply and make list what's needed: Rum, vodka, gin, bourbon, scotch, sherry, bitters, red and white vermouth. More and more people are drinking wine so be sure and have ample of white and red, expecially if you're serving it at dinner. And, of course, there are always those who answer your drink question with a charming, naive smile and say. . . "A daquiri, if it's not too much trouble." Rather than wring her neck have a few bottles of ready mixes handy. . . she'll never know the difference, they never do! Also, beer for some.

Basic Supplies: Cocktail napkins. . . never have enough.

Glasses. . . if possible supplement your own old fashioned hi-ball size glasses with inexpensive dime store varieties; sometimes they are just as cheap or even cheaper in the long run than a lot of plastic glasses. Remember 20 glasses per 14 people.

Tooth picks for pupus, olives, pickled onions, and the usual citrus garbage.

Serving trays and platters.

Ice Ice Ice Ice Ice Ice Ice Ice Ice

Bar equipment: lemon rinder, can openers, wine bottle opener, several jiggers, long stirring spoons, pitcher of water, tea towels, big ice container, slop bowl, green olives, and pickled onions.

Plan Plan Plan Plan Plan Plan Plan
Schedule your time.

The week before the party: Check the china, silver and linen you will be using. Time to borrow or visit better china and silver departments of dime stores! Wash dishes you haven't used for years, polish silver, check linen table cloths and napkins for spots and leave ample time to wash and iron if necessary. Remember! A party is the time to use all of your lovely things! People *do notice!*

If you're using paper napkins instead of linen, be sure and buy the best quality paper. Nothing worse than fingering a shredded, flimsy piece of tissue. If you entertain frequently, invest in monogrammed paper supplies. . . cocktail and dinner napkins and finger tip towels.

Depending on the occasion whip up brite, colorful table cloths. Buy double lengths of material to fit tables, sew up the center and hem the ends. For instance. . . check gingham for red wine, spaghetti and French bread with candles dripping over old wine bottles.

Give the house a general cleaning: A party is not a 'white glove inspection tour', but there are always those who 'sniff and judge'. Inevitably there's always someone who tosses her head back in gales of laughter and stops dead in mid air. . .absolutely fascinated by a lovely cobweb complete with a family of trapped bugs! And, of course, all eyes go ceiling-ward!

How's the medicine chest, darning basket, on-going quilting project, the desk especially where the telephone sits. I mean really! You or I wouldn't poke around, but you just don't know about people! Play it safe!

Check bathroom essentials. . .TP, soap, finger towels. Leave aspirin bottle handy just in case you haven't checked the medicine closet.

Double check traffic hazards: All those doodle-daddle conversation pieces on tables and open shelves. . .preserve those antiques. Not that your friends don't appreciate your beautiful things, but you have heard of bulls in a china shop. Mother's precious plate she bought in Peking umpteen centuries ago can be 'ruins' in one fleeting sweep of an arm.

Put out just enough ashtrays for those few who still persist. Thereby eliminating excuses for dreadful ole butts in your prize potted plants or vases. *Forget about supplying cigarettes!*

Check tired potted plants and replace. . .heaven forbid dusty leaves!

Decide what you're going to wear: You're the star at your party and don't under-dress or over-dress and dismiss that notion of the stunning basic black with granny's pearls. It's a *happy party!* You can have enough time to alter, clean, press or even trot out and buy a new gown.

3 days before the party. Now set up your table for cocktails so you can figure out best flow of traffic to the focal point. Then concentrate on buffet table leaving space in the center for your floral arrangement and maybe candles. Time to set up card tables, too, and borrow, if necessary.

Change whatever furniture needs be for an easy flow of traffic, but don't break your back. . .you still have lots to do! Remember to do something about that antique chair with the broken arm. Inevitably someone always wants to move it or it attracts a 'comfy' 300 pounder like a magnet.

2 days before the party: Now concentrate on your marketing, taking your precious check list and not the piano with you. Buy the *ice*, lots of it and store in freezer. Plan hamburgers for dinner so no leftovers. Preserve precious space in the refrigerator.

Start preparing what foods you can in advance. Smart if you plan your menu to allow this.

Day before the party: If your washing machine is full, run it and clear the decks. You can cool the beer and wine in it!

Buy and arrange flowers. . .be sure and keep your arrangements out of harm's way. Nothing more annoying than gingerly detouring a floor to ceiling creation, stunning as it may be!

While you're out be sure you haven't forgotten anything by checking the list again.

Set up the bar, check needed utensils, leave extra liquor handy.

Continue cooking all that you possibly can.

Arrange plates, silver, wine glasses, and

napkins on tables. Candles? If so, leave them in the freezer until just before using so they'll burn slowly.

Have hot dogs or TV dinners tonight.

Day of party: Relax! Relax! Have your hair done. You can't look exhausted. Double check bathrooms.

Arrange serving dishes on counter or kitchen tables.

Finish last minute cooking.

Have simple supper ready. . . cream tuna and rice. . . for the kiddies and let them watch TV on a school night for once! Strangely enough, there are people who frown on the young, especially with a dog or worse yet a cat in tow, parading through the crowd in sagging pj's munching a chicken bone!

Just before the party. . . don't dwell on "Smarty gave a party and no one came"! Before you know it, there will be so much noise and confusion you won't even be thinking! By all means enjoy your own party. . . you're paying in blood, sweat, tears and dollahs!

MISCELLANEOUS TIPS

You may feel safe inviting a few more than you had planned to as the law of averages works out to 20% 'no-shows'.

Serve hot pupus hot and quickly.

A tempting array of pupus laid out on a large table can stand unattended for eternity. . . neglected. Cocktail party-goers instinctively gather in tight groups and guests would rather starve to death than leave a juicy converstion. Eventually, thank goodness, starvation or faintness drives them to food. . . then *watch out!*

For buffet suppers endear yourself to the gentlemen. Please don't plan a dinner that necessitates knives! Many a handsome trouser has been slit! Try to gear a buffet menu to one dinner plate and a simple dessert and sanka or coffee all on one plate so guests can manage everything easily and not feel like amateur jugglers.

If you're determined to serve soup before supper, have it available around the cocktail center unless, of course, you're having a seated dinner.

Have the bread or rolls buttered and at least warm!

Try to stay posted at the entrance. . . let the guests trip over you coming in and not going out.

Whenever possible do set up tables for at least 3/4 of the guests. Allow ample seating on sofas and chairs complete with coffee tables.

If the weather is threatening, have umbrellas handy and consider a 'shaking off' spot for guests.

If you've asked dear old "Aunt Minnie" be sure, I repeat, be sure and see that no one gets carried away with old-fashioned politeness to elders and sits with her more than fifteen minutes.

A hostess is supposed to have eyes in the back of her head!

Buffet suppers can be the easiest way to entertain for several reasons: everything may be prepared in advance and kept either hot or cold, guests help themselves and the pupus can be ample but simple.

During the hot summer months a completely cold buffet supper serves two purposes; no hot kitchen and no stewing around fretting over the food going cold! Have an assortment of salads. . . potato, salmon mousse, cole slaw, tomato aspic, chicken salad and assorted fruit salads. Platters of cold sliced turkey, tongue or cold cuts and sliced cheeses. Buttered rye bread and they can take their choice. Serve cookies and sanka for dessert.

If you're having a hot supper, keep it warm on warming plates. . . there are always those who loiter.

Cocktail parties with hearty pupus are a great media to check bases with people you haven't seen in years, visiting firemen love being in a home, and obligations can be met gracefully.

If you provide a big pot of hot soup by 8:30 for those who are still enjoying your hospitality, you'll be a roaring success as a hostess and blessed the following morning!

EASTER BRUNCH

Most everyone goes to church Easter Sunday. The kiddies are all hopped up in anticipation of the Easter Bunny and the excitement of the egg hunts and games, and since everyone's all dressed up anyway. . . why not have a festive *Easter Brunch!*

Ask one of your nearest and dearest, and incidentally, the one with the most childern, to take over the egg hunt and events so you are free to concentrate on the prizes and menu.

Plan to set up the bar outside on the lawn or in the patio so that while the young are trampling down your pampered garden beds and gouging the lawn, the elders can be relaxing and happy with a cool libation. However, let the choice be *bloody marys* or *wine* period.

Everyone can help himself. Have available pitchers of ready-mixed tomato juice spiced with lemon juice and herbs and bottles of Worcestershire sauce and tabasco handy for those who love it hot; vodka and gin; lots of ice and glasses. No wavering decisions at this gathering! Beat the pupu problem by serving crisp, strung, stalks of celery and long spears of cucumber with the bloody marys and have baskets of nuts and chips handy. Good idea to have a separate table for the young with gallons of iced *Island Punch* and paper cups.

As for the menu. . . Ham, of course, is traditional, and if you want 'out' from the kitchen, persuade old dad to cook the entree in the kamodo. It's delicious and easy this way. Otherwise, bake it the day before and serve it cold or cook it in time for brunch.

Casseroles of *curried fruit* seem to enhance the ham and can be done well in advance.

Either a casserole of candied yams or macaroni and cheese is delicious with ham and can be done the day before and warmed for serving. Children love the latter, especially, so you could add some ground round as they might just settle for this in all the excitement. Leave these on your electric food warmer on the buffet table and you won't have to run in and out of the kitchen.

Make a Layered Salad day or two before and set it in a large bowl of crushed ice and let it sit, too.

Iced tea and hot coffe and Hot Cross Buns or a Banana Bread should do it. Remember all those wilting jelly beans and mashed candies!

Be sure and provide ample and then some and don't forget the *home made mustard.*

Set your buffet table up outside, too, the day before and have everything ready to go so that when you return from church in your finery you need just remove your hat and enjoy your guests.

If ole dad is an expert ham carver, he'll shave it very thin the way it's supposed to be carved and you won't have the sticky problem of having to have knives. Or you can even serve hot rolls and pop the ham in between.

But remember the cardinal rule. . . no knives for the buffet unless, of course, you provide pretty tables.

Keep your eyes out for Happy Yellow Easter motif paper cups, dishes and napkins. . . being Sunday, no one wants to turn a hand at the sink!

Don't want ham. . . bake a beautiful turkey!

Want alternatives for side dishes? Well, there's *Phoebe's Lima Bean Casserole, Cold Potato Salad, Gabran's Ginger Slaw, Chicken Salad or Namasu.*

Also Onion Cheese Pie, Taro Cakes, Baked Papaya or Bananas. . . and if all this doesn't appeal, use your own favorites!

THE CHRISTENING PARTY

Christenings are happy, happy events and family oriented. Crying or gurgling, the wee-one is always adorable and usually completely lost in the long white ancestral christening gown. The proud parents and godparents beam and repeat their vows. It is customary to invite the older generation and the younger relatives, too, besides a few close friends to the church for the service and to join you at home for refreshments. It needn't be a great production, and actually, the smaller and simpler the better.

Use only your best banquet cloth on the dining room table and have a spring-like bouquet as a centerpiece no matter what time of year. It is a new beginning! Bring out your best cake and dessert plates from the top shelf and your tea napkins that have been sitting in the bottom drawer for years.

The dining room table should be the refreshment center; if you don't have one improvise something that will hold: polished silver or crystal bon bon dishes holding assorted mints, chocolates, and nuts; your special sandwich platter arranged with assorted dainty tea sandwiches (de-crusted and quartered), the heirloom cake plates with slices of rich yellow fruit or banana cake; and fancy dishes with fragile sugar cookies. Good size dessert plates should be stacked at either end. Place your folded tea napkins next to the plates.

At either end of the table or at a separate table have punchbowls with either punch glasses, tumblers or wine glasses to serve a wine punch, ice tea, ice coffee, and a plain fruit punch.

A toast may first be raised to the latest member of the Christian family with champagne. Be sure to have the wine well chilled as well as the glasses. Pour the champagne over ice cubes and a curl of thick orange rind. If you're so inclined keep serving this or concentrate on the wine punch.

Suggestions for sandwiches: watercress and cream cheese, chopped preserved ginger and cream cheese, deviled egg, and plain black chopped olives.

Also easy to make and elegant to behold are small cream puff shells filled with either tuna or chicken mixture.

Always brighten the sandwich trays with dry fresh sprigs of parsley or water cress.

A SHOWER FOR THE BRIDE

It doesn't usually rain in summer. . . but showers, yes, . . for the bride! These special parties for the future bride can be ultra feminine or mixed bag, lavish and grand, or intimate and inexpensive.

Any time of the day is fine if it fits in with the present day's working girl's schedule, unlike the days of yore when the bride had nothing to do but languish in a happy daze, open endless presents and write elaborate thank-you notes at her leisure. . . between parties.

As to the 'shower heads' there are untold angles. . . kitchen, bathroom, bar, personal, set of monogrammed linen (usually given by the bride's mother's friends at today's prices), or miscellaneous.

Unfortunately, the same people tend to be asked to the same pre-nuptial parties and this can become a burden on the budget-conscious young who still have the present to send! A fun and inexpensive way of entertaining is to have a dessert shower with something scrumptious served with coffee or a punch. Ask everyone to bring their favorite recipe nicely typed on a specified size card and one can or bottle of needed ingredient. The hostess can purchase a snappy suitable recipe filing box. Young girls love this shower and come away with great ideas on cooking!

Another girlie-luncheon is to have everyone contributing a dollar to buy some gloriously extravagant whisp of lingerie! It could even be no-host in an inexpensive restaurant with someone ordering the lunch beforehand.

An "Around-the-clock-shower" is great fun for a mixed bag and could be anything from a picnic to a cocktail party. When you ask the guests, specify that they bring something appropriate for certain hours. . . midnight, 1 a.m. and 22 hours thereafter! This stimulates the imagination, is fun and need not be too expensive. For example: 2 tooth brushes and a tube of toothpaste.

Or make it a *wine* or *something for the bar* shower. It's always nice to have a hospitable supply when you first set up housekeeping.

If the bridal couple is moving to another city, have a mixed cocktail party and ask each guest to bring a stamped, self-addressed post card. They could be funny, risque or beautiful! Then if the bride begins to miss old friends. . . she can just pen a quick note.

Whatever you have. . . brunch, luncheon, picnic, tea party, supper or dessert party, do try and plan to allow the bride-to-be lots of time to open all her presents. It is such an exciting time for her. Let her and the donors enjoy all the 'ohs and ahs' and the fancy trimmings.

And don't forget to have paper plates available. . . one for the bride and others for the attendants. Poke a hole in the center and insert all the white ribbons and bows from packages in one and all the colored ribbons and bows in the others.

These will serve as mock boquets the day of the rehearsal, and you'd be suprised how it helps to carry something!

Remember the old wives' tale when opening presents. . . don't have a scissors handy to cut the ribbons! Just let the bride keep untying the knots!

RING AROUND THE HOLIDAYS
THANKSGIVING   CHRISTMAS
NEW YEARS

Thanksgiving and Christmas dinners are traditional. It's a time to give thanks for all our blessings, gather the family and friends round, and for ole *mom* to rise and shine in the kitchen!

In most cases the bird is the piece de resistance at Thanksgiving and it's worth the trouble of ferreting out chilled turkeys! The difference between chilled and frozen is fantastic.

Make the Thanksgiving table festive and damage proof by whipping up a tablecloth in some very autumn-colored inexpensive material with napkins to match. Then you don't cringe when the candles drip on and through the Horn Of Plenty centerpiece.

This is the time, too, when you include single people away from home and those you may not even know too well. In keeping the table on the informal side, everyone can be more relaxed.

In this era of no help in the kitchen, lucky is the one who can still find an extra pair of hands to man the kitchen. If not, make the menu simple but good and ample.

After the blessing on Thanksgiving, you might recite the verse DOTTIE KANEAIA-

KALA'S family always says:
"Gobble, gobble, gobble.
The turkeys are in trobble.
The turkeys are all grieving
Because it's Thanksgeeving."

Acutally you don't need a first course here because this meal is just the formal beginning of a 3-day feast of left-overs!

Suggested menu for Thanksgiving:
Turkey
Rice or Savory Stuffing
Homemade Cranberry Relish
Olives, Celery and Carrot Stix
Cranberry Moulded Salad on Fresh Green
Lettuce Leaves with Sour Cream Dressing
Onion Pie
Zucchini Torte
Peas and Sliced Waterchestnuts
Mashed Potatoes
or
Sweet Potatoes with Marshmallows
Giblet Gravy
Dessert
Mince Pie with Slices of Sharp Cheese
or
Pumpkin Pie. . . with or without ice cream or cream
or
Lilikoi Chiffon Pie
or
All!
Sanka

Be sure to have lots of *chilled white wine*, and keep the glasses tinkling!

At Thanksgiving time in years past the Farden family of Lahaina gathered pumpkins from the fields and Annie Farden made her famous Pumpkin pie. Her daughter, IRMGARD

ALULI says: "She baked her pies in large baking pans. . . about 17x12x5 inches and filled it almost to the top leaving just enough room for the meringue. . . in fact, several pans! Mama's pies were out of this world! The crust must have been at least 2-1/2 inches thick and the edges beautifully fluted."

PUMPKIN PIE

ANNIE FARDEN'S Pumpkin Pie: Mash 1 C cooked pumpkin and mix with 1/2 C sugar, 2 egg yolks and 1 whole egg, 1-1/2 t cinnamon, 1/2 t each ground ginger and lemon extract, and 1 C milk.

Pour in uncooked pie crust and bake in 400 oven for 20 minutes than lower heat to 375. Bake until filling is thick or when inserted knife comes out clean.

Cover with meringue and brown.

SWEET POTATO BALLS

ANNIE FARDEN'S Thanksgiving Sweet Potato Balls.

Mash up sweet potatoes, add a little butter and a beaten egg. Form in shape of small balls evenly around marshmallows. Close up securely, roll in corn flakes and fry in deep fat to brown and heat thru. Drain on brown paper and serve hot.

CRANBERRY ICE

WINONA SEAR'S HUNTER'S Cranberry Ice was a great family tradition that was served along with the big bird. Stew 1 pound fresh cranberries in 1 quart water for 5-10 minutes or until cooked. Strain and add juice of 2 lemons. Sweeten to taste with sugar (it will be tarter when frozen). Freeze in ice cream freezer. Make twice recipe for full freezer.

Winona says it should be done in the ice cream freezer, otherwise it doesn't have the same creamy consistency.

However, Christmas is more a family and elegant dinner time. Do take the time to rustle out your most precious linens and use them! Allow enough time ahead to check, bleach, wash and starch and iron these beautiful cloths and double damask linen napkins. Christmas comes but once a year!

The family remembers these rare occassions and someday they will be referring to this very cloth as 'ole granny's' Christmas banquet cloth.

Be sure you get dripless candles and keep them in the freezer until just ready to use and put in Aunt Minnie's silver candelabra. . . polished to within an inch of its life. Use all your best silver, china and crystal. Red roses for a centerpiece will carry out the holiday colors.

If you've decided not to go the turkey route for Christmas, how about a beautiful *Standing Rib Roast*? Decide on what time you will be sitting down for dinner, and then time and cook it the way you always do and are sure of. Remember it should stand for 20 minutes out of the oven before carving.

Here is a poem by Grace Nole Crowell you might tack up on the refrigerator in early December:

'I shall attend to my little errands of love early this year.

So that the brief days before Christmas may be unhampered and clear.

*Of the fever of hurry. The breathless rush-
ing that I have known in the past*
*Shall not possess me. I shall be calm in
my soul and ready at last for Christmas.*
I shall make leisure.
*I shall not miss the silver silence of the
stars as I have before.*
*And oh! Perhaps. . . if I stand there very
still very long,*
*I shall hear what the clamour of living has
kept from me, The Angel's Song."*

Suggested Christmas Dinner Menu:
*Fresh Fruit Cocktail served in grapefruit
shell baskets topped with a cherry or
mint leaves.*
> *or*
*Clear Consomme with Avocado Balls and
pass crisp bread stix.*
> *or*
*Artichokes Stuffed with Baby Shrimps
and your favorite dressing. Pass Home
made Lavash.*
*Tomato Aspic Salad with Slices of Avo-
cado on Crisp Watercress.*
Roast Beef
Gravy
Yorkshire Pudding
*Baked Potatoes with Sour Cream and
Chives.*
Fresh Steamed Broccoli
Horseradish Mousse
Platter of Olives, Celery and Carrot Stix

Dessert
*Plum Pudding (lit, of course) and Hard
Sauce*
> *or*
Fruit Cake and Hard Sauce or

*Mince Pie with sharp cheese or vanilla
ice cream topping.*
Sanka

This is a festive and very special occassion. . . serve the best red wine you can and
champagne with dessert!

POUND FRUIT CAKE

Here is MARY WILSON'S prize winning
Pound Fruit Cake to make for the holiday season.

In a large bowl and using an electric blender, cream 1 pound butter (if you really want a
pound cake you'll have to use this) with 1
pound (2 C) sugar until really creamy. Then
drop in 8 eggs one at a time and beat well after
each addition. Add 1 t vanilla and 1/2 t lemon
extract.

Before you combine 1 pound (4-1/2 C)
flour with 1 t baking powder, use some of the
flour to sprinkle over 1 pound raisins and 1
pound (1 carton) candied fruit mix and toss
lightly.

With a mixing spoon (or use your hands
like all good cooks) add the flour alternately
with the fruit to the creamed butter, sugar and
egg mixture and combine well.

Pour into two foil-lined loaf pans and
bake at 325 oven for about an hour and 20

minutes. . . but watch and test for inserted tooth pick to come out clean.

Cool and top with slices of large candied red and green cherries to make a merry holiday design.

EGGNOG

Thinking about Eggnog for the holiday season? This is no time to count calories so try this recipe!

Eggnog: In a large bowl let 1/2 gallon of *French Vanilla* ice cream melt, then fold in 1 pint very cold whipped cream. Add 1 pint rum and 1/2 pint brandy or bourbon. Stir, keep well chilled (cradle a smaller bowl on cracked ice in your large punch bowl) and serve in eggnog cups topped with a bit of cinnamon or nutmeg. Makes about 24 cups.

HOLIDAY STUFFED EGGS

DEL BARDWELL makes these Holiday Stuffed Eggs for pupus.

To each dozen egg yolks add 1 can (4-1/2 ounces) drained shrimp and blend well in electric blender or food processor. Add: pepper, dash of curry powder, garlic salt to taste and enough mayonnaise to blend. Adjust seasoning.

With a large star tube fill whites. Soften cream cheese and add some green coloring to tint it. Using the small leaf tube pipe little leaves around yolk filled egg halves.

HOLIDAY FRUIT SQUARES

OLLIE MILLER is famous for her Holiday Fruit Squares she seems to whip up with no effort for friends.

Preheat oven to 375. Grease 9x13x2-1/2 inch baking pan.

Sift 2 C flour with 1 t each baking soda, salt, cloves, 1/2 t cinnamon, 1/8 t nutmeg and set aside.

In a large mixing bowl with wooden spoon or electric mixer at medium speed beat 1/2 C soft oleo with 1-1/4 C flour mixture, blend well, stir in 1 C canned applesauce.

Mix remaining flour mixture with 1/2 C each chopped walnuts and filberts, 1/2 C diced mixed candied fruit, 3/4 C chopped pitted dates and 1/4 C chopped pitted prunes, and add to applesauce mixture. Stir until well blended. Bake 35 minutes or until cake tester inserted in center comes out clean. Cool completely in pan but while still warm cut into squares of 2 inches.

Make decoration: Mix 1-1/2 C sifted confectioners sugar with 2-1/2 T canned cream until smooth. Spread over cake in pan. Decorate with pieces of candied cherries and walnuts.

CHOCOLATE ICE BOX CAKE

PAT HUNTER sent this with a note: "Here is a sinfully delicious, expensive, outrageous dessert we always had at Christmas dinner instead of plum pudding because all of the kids had a sweet tooth, and none of us took much of a fancy to raisins, except in good hot mango chutney."

Chocolate Ice Box Cake: Put 4 squares of bitter chocolate (broken up), 1 C sugar and 1/2 C water in top of double boiler and cook over hot water until blended and smooth.

Beat yolks of 8 eggs until thick and light

and gradually add to chocolate mixture and keep stirring rapidly. Reduce heat and cook until mixture thickens. Remove from heat and cool.

Cream 1 pound butter; add 2 C powdered sugar gradually, stirring constantly, then add chocolate mixture and 1-1/4 t vanilla. Beat thoroughly and fold in the stiffly beaten whites of 8 eggs.

Line the bottom and sides of a 12-inch diameter, 3-1/2 inch deep spring-form pan with waxed paper and brush sides of paper with slightly beaten egg white (to help stick the lady fingers to it).

Line the bottom and sides with lady finger halves (you need about 4-5 dozen). Pour some of the filling into the lady finger lined pan and put more lady fingers in to make a layer of cake, add more filling, and repeat until pan is almost filled and filling is used up. Top with lady fingers.

Refrigerate 24 hours. When ready to serve, turn out onto platter and garnish with sweetened, vanilla flavored whipped cream (you can use Quip).

"You may add pistachio nuts or cherries if you like, but, personally I think that's gilding the lily!" adds Pat.

CHERRY ALMOND LOAVES

CARLA ROBINSON is famous for her Christmas gifts of Cherry Almond Loaves.

Cut 12 ounces glace cherries in half, place in shallow pan and pour 3 ounces of rum over. Let this soak for 1-2 hours.

Let 3/4 pounds of butter melt until very soft in large bowl. Add 3 C sugar and cream well until very fluffy. (Carla uses her hands.) Add 6 eggs beating well after each addition.

Sift 4 C flour with 1 t baking powder and add gradually to butter mixture. You will find that using your hands is easier to mix as it resembles the consistency of short bread and it does take elbow grease to mix.

Sift 1/4 C flour over cherries and add to mixture.

Add 1 (5-1/2 ounce) can slivered almonds. Mix well.

Divide in 6 greased mini loaf pans and bake 60-65 minutes in 300 oven.

These freeze well, too.

NEW YEAR'S EVE IS ANYBODY'S GUESS!

The older you get, the more tempting it becomes to stay right at home and let the gang come to you. It may mean work in the kitchen preparing but then think of it this way. . . you won't have to cook for several days, either! Suggested Buffet Table for New Years Eve:

Platter of variety of Cheese, Breads and Crackers
Pot of Baked Beans
Tossed Greens
Oven Kalua Pork Butt
Mounds of Potato Salad

Pickled Beets
Assorted Pickles and Olives
Molded Salmon Mousse with Sliced Cu-
cumbers and Zucchini with Watercress
    Dressing
Fried Chicken Thighs
Optional
Lau Laus
Lomi Salmon
Poi
Dessert
Use up the Fruit Cake, Nuts, Raisins,
Candies, Etc. Left overs from Christmas.

Sparkling Burgundy is great to serve, especially at midnight! Keep the washing machine full of cold beer and wine! Never know who'll pop in!

Honolulu Advertiser

....Articles....

MEMORY TIME

With Thanksgiving in mind it occurred to me that in the olden days and even in our childhood, the old-time Hawaiians were constantly giving thanks for all their blessings.

As children we never sat down to a meal with our *kupunas* (elders) without a blessing that seemed to go on and on and on. . . and all in Hawaiian. Each time the dear soul stopped for a breath or dropped his voice, we opened one eye to see if we could begin eating the food that was fast getting cold.

However, his solemn expression and prayerful hands indicated otherwise, and we closed our eyes and tried to forget food and concentrate on a familiar word. Hawaiians gave thanks for each and every blessing, and not just for the food.

The Hawaiians had *mana*. . . divine power. . . and great inner peace that came from living with their God in a tranquil land.

Probably the original formal Thanksgiving of the Hawaiians goes back to the *makahiki* which lasted from November to February. The time being determined by the tides and moon.

What a tremendously joyous time it was, too! No *hana-hana* (work). . . no *kaua* (wars).

Rather than referring to it as tax-time, these fun-loving ancient Hawaiians referred to it as a time of giving thanks with offerings to the king. Gifts of the finest *tapa*, sea shells, feather work, sweet potatoes, *taro*, and other fruits of the land were all offered to *Lono*, God of Plenty.

Once the temple priests visited the altars with prayers of thanksgiving and blessed the land and people, spontaneous celebrations broke forth. . . a grand *ho'olaulea*! Great sports, war games, fabulous feasts, much singing and dancing and merriment ensued.

As a climax the king had to prove himself worthy of representing the God Lono. It was time for the testing of the spears. Out to sea he paddled in his regal outrigger canoe, returned to shore and braved the onslaught of warrious rushing at him with raised spears.

If he defended himself successfully against this deadly assualt, his kingly rights were restored and he gave thanks, thereby bringing the annual thanksgiving festival to a victorious and glorious finale.

Then it was the missionaries' turn to celebrate Thanksgiving but not necessarily at the same time the folks back home did.

The first company of missionary families from New England arrived on the brig *Thaddeus* and celebrated their first Thanksgiving in the Hawaiian Islands on December 2, 1820.

Lucy Goodale Thurston wrote her father in Massachusetts. . . "We had not that rich variety but we had enough of that which was good, viz, roast pork, meat pie, biscuit and cheese."

In the book, *"Lowell and Abigail"* written by their granddaughter, Mary Dillingham Frear, there is a letter from Mrs. Lowell Smith to her family dated December 6, 1838.

"This day has been observed by us missionaries and people of Honolulu as a day of Thanksgiving and praise to Almighty God.

"An interesting day. . . seemed like old times. . . Thanksgiving in the United States. As a mission we have been abundantly blessed in spiritual things. Several thousand have been hopefully converted."

King Kamehameha III set the first official Thanksgiving Day in Hawaii as December 31, 1849, but in 1860 the Hawaiian Evangelical Association successfully campaigned for a November Thanksgiving.

These excerpts from a Thanksgiving speech delivered in Hawaiian in a local church in 1897 may well be repeated today.

"We give thanks for: immuntiy from all kinds of disease; the blessing of peace; the plentiful food and for never having known the horrors of starvation; and for no floods."

And when you gather round that plump, browned bird. . . just remember to give a silent prayer of thanks to dear ole *Kaahumanu*, for it was she who first noticed the strange bird on board Capt. John Meek's ship in Kailua Bay in 1815.

Unfortunately she mentioned it to Kamehameha, whereupon he paddled out to the ship and called to Capt. Meek demanding the strange bird.

The captain's protesting that he had given the bird to Kaahumanu came to naught. He lost to the powerful Kamehameha who demanded his prey and paddled gleefully back to shore with a gobble-gobble here and a gobble-gobble there.

As a matter of fact, their song has echoed down the ages. . . "Gobble, gobble, gobble. . . The turkeys are in trouble. . ."

Happy, Happy Thanksgiving!

CHRISTMAS IS NOSTALGIA TIME

As the Christmas season approaches so many memories seem to waft back across the years!

Christmas Eve was the time for seranading. Handsome Hawaiian lads garbed in white flannels and white silk shirts strolled along with their *ukuleles* and guitars singing the old Hawaiian favorites for *aloha!* They wore the aromatic *hala lei* entwined with pungent *maile*. How those boys could sing and harmonize just for the love of singing! You never knew when they would drop by but whenever it was you rose to the occasion.

Besides the lovely permeating scent of the Christmas tree, the house was awash with the spicy scent of *maile*. . . *leis* were festooned around pictures, over grandfather clocks or swagged over doorways and stairways. Tables held trays of assorted nuts, raisins, tangerines and crab apples, and the colorful ornate Chinese paper boxes of dried *lychee* nuts were a decoration in themselves.

A *kamaaina* family with eight children had a famous chef, Harry, who always outdid himself at Christmas. How vivid it all is to this day. . . that bigger than life size Santa Claus Harry created and stuffed with all sorts of goodies and presents for the children gathered round.

It was a lark to make the trek up into the mountains to gather *wawae-iole* (mouse foot), a creeping moss-like plant, to fashion Christmas wreaths. The addition of a few bunches of the red Hawaiian Christmas berries, a big red bow and the front door was decorated. Simple!

Christmas Eve was usually the time for the big dinner and Hawaiian homes never lacked for groaning boards! There was always house-hold help and a major domo in the kitchen. New Year's was their big holiday and time to celebrate.

The kitchen was the hub of the house in the days preceding the 25th. The menu revolved around a large fresh chilled turkey with the usual bread stuffing 'plucked' from several day-old loaves. Creamed cauliflower, peas, creamed onions and sweet potatoes were standard.

For good measure a leg of fresh island pork or pork butt was roasted in the oven to a crisp turn, *poi* was mixed in large bowls several days in advance so as to be just right. . . not too fresh and not too sour. . . and jars of *lomi*

salmon were prepared with green onions cleaned and wrapped in wax paper. And always a gorgeous potato salad riddled with hard boiled eggs and fresh parsley and a pot of old Boston baked beans!

The table featured the finest of cut-work linen cloths, silver, crystal and china, and the first course was invariably grapefruit or papaya baskets filled with a minted icy cold fruit cocktail. A salad of crispy fresh Manoa lettuce, pomelo and avocado with French dressing was set before you while Papa carved the mammoth bird lei-d with a string of cranberries.

Then it was up to you to help yourself at the gourmet buffet table and decide which route to go! Those beans, potato salad, and cold turkey sure hit the spot the next day after eggnogs!

Older and wiser (?) today I know that as children we ate much too much cake. . . but with great intent and purpose! Somewhere in that batter had been baked a ring, a thimble, numerous dimes and various treasures. (Maybe today it's the same joy children find in those gum machines!)

Fruit cakes and plum puddings were made in October or November and aged in fine old brandy. If you've never broken down suet or de-seeded golden raisins for a real old fashioned plum pudding you just haven't lived. And that real butter hard sauce piled temptingly in the best crystal cut glass dish! And then the apex of the whole exciting evening. . . when the lights were turned off and in came the flaming plum pudding held high midst great pomp and circumstances!

Actually, to go back even further the first recorded Christmas in Hawaii was in 1786 when an English sea captain aboard the *Queen Charlotte* anchored in Waimea Bay, Kauai, celebrated with a bowl of punch, roasted pig, seapie and toasts to friends and family in England.

Seventy-six years later in 1862 King Kamehameha IV proclaimed Christmas day a national holiday in Hawaii. On Christmas Eve the churches of Honolulu were ablaze with candlelight for the midnight services. After the services at the Episcopal cathedral, the king and Bishop Staley headed a procession of torch bearers and a vested choir. They then marched through the streets singing Christmas hymns and ended at the old palace where fireworks were set off and the king and queen acknowledged Christmas greetings from the people.

And so it has been. . . *Mele Kalikimaka!*

CHRISTMAS IN HAWAII THROUGH WAR AND PEACE

It's time for the Feast of the Christmas Spirit!

Under balmy skies Hawaii has welcomed Christmas from monarchy through provisional government, republic, territory, war with its martial law, and statehood.

The great Christian anniversary was first officially observed and adopted as a national public holiday in 1860. Kamehameha IV and Queen Emma participated in the Christmas eve service. . . the first attempt to popularize the celebration of Christmas in this land.

Mrs. John Dominis, mother-in-law of Queen Liliuokalani, is credited with bringing the traditional Christmas trees to Honolulu.

A transplanted Bostonian, she brought many New England customs with her. She built the mansion on Beretania Street and named it Washington Place to remind her of her homeland. She was famous for her beautifully decorated Christmas trees and festive boards.

From the time of their arrival, the protestant missionaries quietly observed Christmas day with the usual religious services.

One of the earliest missionary familes started a custom that became a great family tradition. . . The Cooke Family Christmas Breakfast.

"In the early days the Breakfast was held at Grandma Cooke's (Mrs. Charles M. Cooke, Sr.)" recalls her grandaughter, Dora Derby.

"All the aunties volunteered their domestic help. In latter years, caterers were engaged, one family member ordered the groceries, and each family donated money toward the total cost.

"In earlier times the Montague Cookes always supplied Mother's Muffins, a special recipe from Granny Lefferts, Aunt Lila's mother.

"George and Sophie Cooke provided the turkeys which they raised on Molokai. For two weeks before the turkeys were killed they were confined in a very small pen and fed a diet of cracked corn and sour milk. The quality of their meat was memorable!

"Grapefruit was traditional, but papaya was substituted when grapefruit couldn't be obtained on account of World War II.

"The number of family members frequently went over a hundred. The seating was never prearranged and everyone usually sorted themselves roughly into age groups. The Doxology was sung in lieu of grace, then everyone fell in.

"Unfortunately, the last Cooke family

Christmas Breakfast was held December 25, 1967 at Theodore and Muriel Cooke's home on Makiki Heights. Fifty-four were present. The year before there had been 85. . . considerably less than the count in the '50's.

"The menu consisted of papaya and orange juice, creamed turkey on toast points; cranberry sauce; potato chips; English muffins with butter, jelly and marmalade, coffee for adults and milk for children.

"After the meal a traditional game of lawn bowls, senior members vs. the younger fellows, took place.

"And so we would end an opportunity to catch up on cousin's children and grandchildren, family news, etc. etc." concluded Dora with a whisper of sadness in her voice.

Maybe some day one of the *moopunas* will have a home big enough to recall the troops . . . sure hope so!

Retired Navy Capt. Wilfred J. Holmes may have been a bit vague on whether it was a tall limb of ironwood decked out with stars, angels, candles and ribbons, or a *Kamani* tree branch. But he remembered the war-time Christmases vividly!

"Nineteen-forty-one? It was a grim Christmas. I was luckier than most men." said Jasper.

"I had a few hours at home to cover the windows of a small room with heavy building paper, so that my wife and son would have one place where a light could be turned on at night.

"The families of men who were at sea in submarines and carriers were waiting evacuation to the Mainland and our house was a refuge for some of them.

"They all probably had Christmas dinner together there. I do remember that we had to take Eric's Christmas present, a puppy, early as the mother dog was evacuated to the Mainland several days before.

"I had to be back at Pearl Harbor before sunset for no one wanted to be on that blacked-out road at night and brave the jittery patrols.

"Everyone was more apprehensive when the sun went down and all Hawaii withdrew into a primitive, unbroken darkness.

"Mistaking shadows on the waves for approaching landing craft in the surf, nervous sentries frequently would open up with machine gun fire, and start an alarm that spread from post to post.

"Each morning before dawn, search planes took off, laboring over the house-tops to lift their heavy loads of fuel, for the long day's search for enemies in Hawaii's blue skies and shimmering seas.

"That Christmas morning, Adm. Chester W. Nimitz arrived from the Mainland by flying boat.

"A whaleboat carried him ashore across Pearl Harbor, thick with oil from sunken ships, past boats still loaded with bodies that had been dredged from the wrecks, past the sunken and broken *Arizona*, that had been his flagship only three years before.

"Through it all he maintained the aura of calm confidence and strength from which everyone who knew him drew hope and courage. No one could forsee that within six months the despondence of defeat would be dispersed by the brilliant victory at Midway.

"Every other Christmas during the war we had as many 'bachelors' as the house would hold for a sit-down turkey dinner, but not in 1941!"

How quickly we pick up the pieces, forget, and carry on.

The horn of plenty has tumbled forth generously for people from many lands, walks of life, circumstances, creeds and races. And from these fabled Hawaiian Islands, Christmas cheer and kind and loving thoughts go out to all the world!

Peace on Earth and good will towards men.

RING IN THE NEW

Those who only remember Fort Street as one way or as The Mall, will have to shut their eyes tight and try to picture it as it was in 1901 when Charles James Day opened his store on the *ewa* side of the street.

Traffic flowed both ways, and street car tracks down the middle ran from the foot of Fort St. to Beretania, left to Nuuanu and ended at the Country Club road.

On the Waikiki side between Hotel and King streets were Benson Smith Drug Store, Warren's Photo Co., Bergstrom Music, Bill Smith's Manufacturer Shoe Store, Lycurgus restaurant and ice cream parlor and McInerny shoe store. On the *ewa* side were Detor's Jewelry, Gurry's Art Shop, C.J. Day, Hollister's Drug, H.F. Wichman's jewelry store and the one and only department store later called Liberty House.

Reminiscing with Kenneth Day was joyous. I so vividly remember shopping on Fort St. with my mother and being intrigued by all the goodies in C.J. Day's windows! Especially, the elaborate bon bons we coveted on special occasions for their loud 'crackers', paper hats, trinkets and fortunes! Bins of alligator pears and open crates of fresh potato chips imported from San Francisco and dispensed by hand into bags lined the entrance. It was the place to shop for gourmet foods and specialties besides staples.

"Father had very definite ideas," Kenneth Day recalled. "Never sell anything you wouldn't feed to mother. . . get rid of it, throw it away! When you weigh anything always weigh up to the weight and if the arm goes over a few ounces people will think they're getting something *manawahi* whereas if you overload and take away! And once you've let a lady handle a food package it's two-thirds sold!

"Father never carried two things. . . alcoholic beverages or tobacco. Soon after he died, the gray-haired president of the W.C.T.U. burst into the store. . . 'Kenneth, whatever are you doing with a display of wine jelly in the window!' I soon placated her with the promise of several cases to see if she'd get a headache!

"All the *kamaaina* families in the islands traded with us. Princess Kawanakoa loved to shop from her Pierce Arrow parked at the curb. Queen Liliuokalani's orders were promptly filled and delivered to Washington Place. Prince Cupid and his wife, Kahanu, frequently came in together and their purchases were delivered to their Waikiki home which is now the site of Kuhio Park. The famous cateress, Mabel Beckley, always bought delicacies for her parties from us. Doris Duke was a steady customer when in residence at her Shangrila at Kaalawai.

"We were very proud of our top quality specialties. Our coffee was made from beans aged three years then roasted, ground and packaged by the Wing Coffee Company. It was sold under our exclusive label... 'Day's Kona Coffee from Hawaii... it's good if it comes from Day's'. A pound carton sold for 35 cents or three pounds for a dollar. Beans aged for five years sold in five pound tins were more delectable and expensive. I remember my mother brewing coffee in the open gray enamel pot for about 5 minutes, dropping in the egg shells, then dribbling cold water over the top to settle the grounds.

"My father's brother was a tea taster in Ceylon and perfected Kurenwatte Ceylon Orange Pekoe. It was packaged with our label in Ceylon.

"We imported Palm Leaf Butter, the highest grade available in New Zealand, under our label. We introduced Ritz Crackers, Frango Mints, and Armour's canned hams. It was also a delicatessen, with mammoth 176 pound wheels of cheese from Switzerland. I made a special point of cutting off a pound of Swiss with lots of *pukas*... the more *pukas* the better the quality... for a charming lady. But she protested, 'No, no. I'm not paying for a pound of *pukas!* I want cheese.' Reluctantly I cut a pound from the inferior side which hadn't fermented to create the *pukas*.

"Our gift baskets were popular and in great demand on steamer days and around holidays. Ranging in price from $5.00 to $6.00, it included all sorts of specialties imported from around the world... Malaga raisins on the stems from Spain, a 4-ounce jar of Bolegua Malasol Caviar... $1.95 compared to $15.00 today... anchovies, green olives stuffed with almonds, 'water thins' biscuits from Carr's in England, and boxes of glaze fruits I personally selected and ordered in Fresno California. We never used pineapple!

"How we loved it when shy romantic couples came in to order their 'honeymoon baskets'!' We began from essentials and worked right through the most delectable items to last them for two weeks.

"Outside islanders depended on us to fill their Christmas orders and place them aboard the Inter-Island ships. One evening at choir practice I heard the 9 o'clock whistle of the *Waialeale* and my voice froze! I was sure the Knudsen boxes were sitting in the store! I called Stanley Kennedy, founder and president of Hawaiian Airlines, and asked if he would possibly take the boxes on his early morning plane. 'We don't do this type of thing, Kenneth, however, buy a seat and have it at the airport at 6 a.m. and we'll do it for you.' He always intimated to me that this might have been the start of inter-island air freight!

"I always enjoyed doing business with one so punctilious as Gen. George Patton, then stationed at Fort Shafter. Always immaculately dressed in khaki breeches with polished boots and carrying his swagger stick, he would climb the ladders to get what he wanted from the top shelves, amass an order, look at me, then his watch and say, 'I'll be back at... 3... 29!' His order was immediately filled and placed in his red convertible parked in the rear ready and waiting because he drove off at 3:29!

"One day I watched a very pretty woman obviously admiring the window display. She looked so familiar. She came in and I showed her our beautiful Hawaiian gift packages of jams, jellys, coffee and paper *ilima lei*. My, she was so pretty, and I finally asked if we had met before. She smiled and said, 'Well, no. I don't believe formally. I am Mary Pickford.'

"A very dapper man walked in asking for me. 'They tell me,' he began straight away, 'that you can answer any question I might have. Who is the best deep sea fisherman around here?' I walked him down to E.O. Hall to meet Jim Harvey. Your name, sir? 'Zane Grey.'

"And we had lots of local color in those days, too. When a rare hail storm pelted Fort St., two little Hawaiian boys were dumbfounded and one exclaimed. . . 'Auwe, Akua he make shave ice!'

"Fortuitiously, my lease on the store ran out in 1943. I could see the handwriting on the wall. . . big supermarket chains were coming into Hawaii. Cash and Carry! Gone were the days of delivering a 5 cent loaf of bread and a cake of soap to Waikiki! It had been a way of life we shared with all the best in Hawaii for 42 years! God Bless them!"

TIPS FOR TOURIST TIME

This is the time of year when letters start dribbling in from the likes of an old school chum you haven't heard from in umpteen years, what's more seen since the class reunion back when! She's coming out to the islands. . . with her husband. . . oh, so full of enthusiasm!

"Can't wait to catch up with you, Dahling, and share a bowl of *poi* and fresh fish! Been dreaming of this for years now and now that Frank and I..."

Or maybe it's short. . . "Dear One, I know you'll absolutely adore the Rights. They live next door and we've known them for years. Hope you don't mind. . ."

And if you live quietly on an outside island you really hit the jackpot!

You can try putting these letters aside, forget about it, pretend you're off the island, dismiss those pricks of conscience. Then you begin to wonder what the new husband's like, and after all she and ole John were kind to us when we went through Timbuktu 10 years ago. . . and then back even further!

In the good old days such letters were few and far between. Ships only arrived once a week, there were only a few hotels on the beach at Waikiki, traffic was no problem, and household help abounded.

Steamer day was a great occasion for everyone and what was one more *lei* for a stranger! You could always enjoy the Royal Hawaiian Band music and soloists while waiting for new friends under XYZ in luggage.

Lovely to drive them up to Tantalus and show off the sleepy city below. Even more fun to drive around the island stopping at Cooper Ranch Inn for fabulous Planter's Punches and delicious luncheons. And, of course, a *poi* supper was one of the nicest ways to entertain the visitor. It was all part of what was called the Aloha Spirit. . . the *kamaaina's* pleasure to share the charm of their islands!

However, gone are the ships, up goes more concrete, in zoom the planes, no one wants to drive that airport route at peak hours and as for *leis!*

But the *poi* supper is still the way to entertain, if only for a few, and not half the 'bah and humbug' one imagines involved. Actually, the table decor and amassing the many wooden and crystal dishes is more time-consuming. Today's hostess can cook up a *poi* supper and freeze ahead of time and tend to the fun details the day of the party.

A delicious menu that will impress your ole friends includes: Kalua Pork, recipe on page 50, Lomi Salmon, page 57, Poi, and maybe some baked bananas, page 133 and fish wrapped in *ti* leaves, page 56. One cannot forget the haupia for dessert.

Before the party day "eye" your neighbor's flower garden, order *ti* leaves from the florist unless you have a friend with *ti* leaves growing wild. If possible lay a 'cloth' of overlapping fresh clean *ti* leaves down the table. Alternative could be *palaka* or *tapa* material.

Once the 'cloth' is down, lay fresh mountain ferns down the middle and then begin arranging the flowers or fruits. Any island flowers will do but pompons of plumeria blossoms are attractive. . . stick toothpicks in each blossom and then completely cover heads of cabbages. Or weave, string, or sew *leis* to twine down the center of the table. Whole pineapples with centers cut out and cored are stand-bys, likewise the watermelon sliced Van Dyke style. But this is the fun and creative part!

However, remember to leave lots of room for the individual dishes. . . crystal wine glasses and finger bowls with rose geranium leaves floating, coconut or glass dishes for the condiments, chicken, pork, salmon, *poi*, and fish. Haupia and bananas and potatoes can be strewn around on *ti* leaves. Linen napkins a must, but you won't have to worry about polishing the flatware. . . you don't use it!

A LEISURELY DAY WITH THE FAMILY AROUND THE IMU

The whole idea of a day around an *imu* may be staggering but not if you have a mini-*imu*. Of course, it helps to have friends who will lend you those special pourous river rocks (or you have access to a dry stream bed) and supply ample *ti* leaves, banana trunks and leaves.

You also need gunny sacks, and *kiawe* or guava wood or charcoal, but plenty of. But it's fun, fun. . . and worth it all! It can involve the whole family and give ole mom a break. Simple. Just throw everything into the pit, close it for four hours, have some fun and then feast on your labors.

That's the large print and then we come to the fine print and nitty-gritty. Think of it all this way. . . we're going to have a family outing and a feast the way the natives used to cook and save electricity to boot.

For starters, forget a pig and try a turkey. *Imu:* Dig a *puka*, 3x3x2, in the ground (you'll be happier if you find a spot with loose dirt or sand to spade up), have a lot of good firewood, and lay a nice *big* fire then light it up. When the roaring fire begins to settle down to a good rolling burn, spread it out and pile on the rocks. . . only the porous river rocks now or they'll explode.

This is the secret to *imu*-cooking: the fire has to be raging hot with long-lasting intense heat for those rocks to retain the heat properly. Takes quite a while for them to reach the proper heat, but you'll know they're ready when they turn gray then white. Now spread out a nice little bed of those white rocks and coals. . . sure the rocks are fiery hot!

Place a halved, smashed banana trunk on the bed, next banana leaves, and then a top sheet of *ti* leaves. Now tuck the well-buttered bird in for his final nap which should take about 3-4 hours. Cover him by pulling up the covers around him. . . the *ti* and banana leaves. Oh, you'll need help doing this, all right.

Then with those trusty tongs push more hot stones all around to keep him really hot, pile on more wet banana and *ti* leaves, cover the whole with layers of damp burlap, and cover this completely with enough dirt so that not one vapor of steam can escape.

(Sorry but I must digress because at this point I always remember those 'fly boys' based at Pearl during World War II, who returned to New York and decided to impress their sophisticated friends. After they had successfully covered the *imu*, they withdrew indoors for a well-earned drink. Would you believe an unexpected snow fell and it was days before they found the piglet!)

Anyway, back to the turk. After you're sure no steam is escaping, go for a swim but don't get cleaned up, there's more to come. After four hours, get out the gloves, and keep a pan of cold water handy for dipping.

Shovel off the dirt, *care-ful-ly* peel back the burlap and leaves. . . don't want mud in the bird's eyes. Voila. . . the bird, maybe a bit white, but juicy and with a unique flavor. Save the juices in the bottom leaves and use for gravy.

After all this a pig's a cinch.

It may not be carrying out the Hawaiian theme but everybody loves a hearty potato and tossed green salad, and/or a pot of real old-fashioned baked beans. Minted spears of pineapple will top it all off.

THINK PICNIC

Decided to give a picnic? Great idea. What fun!.

Of course you're taking for granted that it will be gorgeous weather, no rain, a full moon even, and you've always been able to grab your favorite picnic site before!

Picnics are simple. . . hamburgers or hot dogs, lots of cold salad, maybe hot baked beans . . . everyone just loves a picnic!

You're delighted. . . all 20 guests can come Saturday evening around four. You weren't planning to take your kiddies but the Bratts have to bring theirs. . . they just love to swim and my dear, they're really no trouble at all!

And now for the logistics.

You'll have to know exactly where you're going. . . the exact spot so everyone will meet at the proper site and not be over the next sand dune.

You'll need: collapsible tables, some folding chairs would be nice, too, and oh, yes, cloths for the tables. Lots of ice, borrow a few ice chests. . . lugging those heavy things to the fun spot will really be worth it.

You spend a small fortune in supplies but there'll be no cleaning up of dishes! Lots of paper plates of various dimensions, lots of napkins, plastic forks, knives, spoons, glasses, hot and cold cups, kitchen utensils and serving spoons. "Off" cans for the bugs, few beach mats to strew around might be comfy, too, especially when Tom brings out his guitar, and why not some pillows! Musn't forget the big garbage bags. . . don't want to be a litter bug!

Couple of cases of beer should do it. . . bring a big container to keep it cold, too. Maybe just a bottle or two of vodka and bourbon along with the mixes. . . but then so many people are drinking wine these days. Better pack along a few whites and reds, you never know their preference.

And now for the menu. Well, we'll have to take a grill for the hamburgers and hot dogs. Two kinds of buns, butter, mustard, hot and regular, ketchup, relish, salt and pepper, pickles.

Potato salad or baked beans. . . folks love them both. Well, let's have both, by all means! No problem making the salad the night before and anyway beans taste so much better left to mellow a few days.

Tossed green salad simple. . . just clean lots of lettuce at home, rinse, dry and put in cellophane bag but keep cold and have dressing. Yes, way ahead of time can do this.

Dessert? They all love Brownies and so easy to whip up several pans!

Coffee or sanka. . . couple of thermoses will keep well and you can always borrow some, too. Cream and sugar?

Flashlights and lanterns. That should be about it!

And then something happens on the way to the picnic. Papa gets in the act! "Over my dead body will I tote all that stuff a quarter of a mile!"

So you end up calling the Bratts and cancelling the kiddies and asking everyone to come over to the patio for a very, very informal barbecue and for goodness sake come comfortable. And bless good ole Batty Bratts. . . she suggested sending your kids to their house and splitting the baby sitter's fee!

After all, people love to visit informally and the men can gather round the grill and the ladies can exchange recipes! Net result. . . you've given a great party and everyone had a good time including ole Pops!

But like it or not, if you have children at home you're going to have to organize a picnic now and then. So why not do it the (it says here) painless way?

If you keep a running picnic basket ready at all times there's no problem. Have it filled with: paper napkins, plates, cups, plastic forks, spoons and knives, salt and pepper, packaged ice tea mix, a sharp kitchen knife and a can opener. A light styrofoam cooler holds a lot besides the ice.

There are simple picnic fares that you could whip up in a few minutes and just take off. . . and I don't mean peanut butter and jelly and a loaf of bread!

Grab a can of corned beef, empty into bowl and add chopped onions (if family is so inclined), ketchup, relish, mayonnaise, mustard and dill, mash it all around and put in plastic carton. Throw in a package of Saloon Pilots, jar of pickles, a few six-pacs and soda pops and you're off! Ice cream always hits the spot on the way home.

How's about roasting up a nice little chicken. . . capon? . . . the day before? Wrap it in foil, butter a loaf of good sour dough bread, throw some white wine in the cooler with ice along with some cleaned crispy lettuce and whole tomatoes. . . or even cooked chicken parts for the kiddies to grab on the run. . . and you're off and running!

Then there's always the apples, cheese and nut routine!

If you invest in oneof those portable fold up barbecue broilers some genius thought up, you then can take along prepared hamburgers, hot dogs and buns, etc. Why do they always taste so much better at the beach?

Somewhere in between the likes of Ward McAllister's Newport society picnics which featured partridges, pate, hams and game pies washed down with champagne and served at glittering tables by servants galore. . . and the old Hawaiian favorite of canned salmon, raw onions and *poi*. . . somewhere there is a happy medium!

Remember picnics are fun! Sand or no sand!

TAKING A ROYAL TOUR

How lucky can you be! Jim Bartels gave me a sneak preview of Iolani Palace! Met him at the kitchen steps of the palace to '*nana*' around the royal kitchen and ended up two hours later with the grand tour from basement to turrets. . . in another world of history, memories, polished koa wood, crystal chandeliers and fantastic restoration work!

The moat which surrounds the basement area rather sets the building apart in its own domain and lets the sunlight and air stream through the big basement windows.

The *mauka* steps to the basement served as the delivery and servants' entrance to the kitchen. The first thing you see as you enter is a tremendous food safe for storage of fruits, vegetables, canned goods, flour, sugar, rice and the likes.

Along the right wall six or more barrels of *poi* were delivered and stored. The chamberlain's ledger accounts for daily delivery of *poi* at 3/4 cents per pound, along with great quantities of canned corn beef and salmon.

The kitchen proper isn't too large a room and has an adjoining scullery area with a huge copper sink, the only one, actually. The *Friends of Iolani Palace* are hoping some kind souls will donate a wood burning stove to fill a large hooded void, which originally held two stoves, one of which they already have.

The restoration architects were able to reproduce floor to ceiling cabinets along one wall, next to the two dumbwaiters which serviced the main dining room above and the family dining hall on the second floor.

We could imagine chefs ladling steaming concoctions into great silver tureens, ready for hoisting to the butler's pantry to be wheeled with great bravado to the elegantly set dining tables.

The whole basement area is almost completed and the renovation leaves nary a trace of the cluttered filing rooms and offices of the old Senate days. The hallway running the width of the palace downstairs is very spacious and was used for *luaus* by Queen Liliuokalani.

Off this hallway are storage rooms for the quilts, feather capes, and *kahilis*, trunks, china, silver, linens, and crystal. . . and when you think of seventy dozen champagne glasses alone, you begin to grasp the enormity of it all!

The *Ewa* stairs to the basement lead to the hub of all official business, the Chamberlain's suite of offices on the right. Kalakaua's two private store rooms are on the left. We talked of Curtis Iaukea, Charles H. Judd, George W. Macfarlane and James Robertson, who in their day, ran the palace from this office.

The Chamberlain attended to details of the king's day, ordered invitations and menus to be printed, controlled the servant life and activity, met at conference tables with callers, and managed all details of palace life. Outside of his office is an anteroom for people on official business and a large room which housed the staff of bookkeepers and messengers. An old style telephone on the wall is evidence that the palace was one of the first to house Mr. Bell.

The Waikiki entrance was used by the Royal Guard and by Queen Liliuokalani as a private entrance and exit. There are no basement steps under the front entrance, and this area was used as the laundry.

Triple sinks have been duplicated, and from the looks of them that job had to be one of the more menial ones in the palace. There are giant hooks from the ceiling for the clothes line, but it's a wonder any laundry dried in that dank part of the basement. Maybe the queen's *holokus* with their long trains hung from there.

Hawaiian royalty ate well. When the Duke of Edinburgh was feted in 1869 in the first Iolani Palace, for starters there was turtle soup with sherry or Soup a la Reine.

The fish course was listed as boiled and fried and washed down with a moselle. Champagne was served with a choice of entree from Totelettes a la boulbais, sweet breads and brown sauce, oyster pates and mutton chops with vegetables.

During the roast course, the wine stewards were dispensing hock, claret and burgundy along with the sirloin beef, leg of boiled mutton, veal, ham, roast turkey, pigeon pie, wild ducks, rice and curry.

Vegetables consisted of asparagus, French peas and beans, tomatoes, green corn, boiled *taro*, sweet potatoes, Irish potatoes, etc. etc., ending with macaroni. For a grand finale Madeira and port were served with cabinet puddings, raspberry coconut puddings, currant pie, tarts, raisins and almonds, jellies, cheese cake, custard and blanc mange. At the very bottom of this gastronomic fanfare was printed "Fruits", in bold letters.

Just a plain old menu gave you a choice of either turtle or mullagatawny soups: for fish, *kumu*, crabs or mullet. For entrees. . . salmi of duck, lawalued pigeon and cutlets. Roasts seemed rather skimpy with only a choice of chicken or beef a la mode. . . or shrimp curry. A choice of cheese with salad, and for dessert Iolani pudding, jelly, fruit cake, ice cream and tea or coffee. (Where were the wine stewards?)

And remember, the chef couldn't take a can of frozen coconut milk from a freezer for his puddings. . . they started from scratch. The coconut was grated, mixed with hot milk or water and then the rich milk was extracted by straining through fine cloth.

The lawalued pigeon sounds intriguing. Since there are no records of any palace recipes we'll just have to wonder if the bird was wrapped in *ti* leaves like fish and baked or wrapped in *luau* leaves then *ti* leaves like a *laulau* and steamed.

Could Iolani Pudding be coconut milk sweetened to taste, mixed with mashed bananas and a little pearl tapioca, baked and served like bread pudding? Or was it sweet potato pudding made by skinning and grating 6 large sweet potatoes and mixing with 1-1/4 pints of coconut milk, pinch of sugar and salt, and placing it in well buttered baking dish to bake in slow oven for 1 hour?

But then, some of the good cooks today still prefer this method!

Since they used so much coconut in those days and gin was so popular wonder if Iolani Punch was simply the milk of the young coconut mixed with gin.

PALACE HAPPENINGS

A tale of two 19th century happenings. . . one a joyous party at Iolani Palace, the other, a grim account of the stripping of the Palace and selling out the royal elegance. . . comes to light in a pair of clippings from the old Pacific Commercial Advertiser.

The first story, under the dateline Feb. 22, 1892, was headlined *"Children's Ball. Her Majesty (Queen Liliuokalani) Entertains About 80 Of The Young Folk. The Throne Room The Scene of A Unique Party."*

"The Children's Fancy Dress Ball was one of the most delightful which eye ever looked on in this little kingdom.

"The palace was bright with electric lights, the large hall, the throne, reception and dining rooms tastefully decorated with flowers, when the carriages began to file into the west gate in a long line.

"The little costumed creatures came dancing up the steps accompanied by their mamas, who for once were thrown in the shade."

Here are only a very few names from the guest list (and their choices of costume): Allison Jordan, Lord Fauntleroy; Henry Alexander Walker, Highland Chief; Cordelia Bishop Walker (Dunkhauser), Highland Chiefess; Linda Schaefer (Castle), Fairy Cupid; Freddie Iaukea, Colonel; Juliet King (Kimball), Snow; Edward Newmann, Signor Hangiapolenta Spaghetti; Charles O. Berger, a Buckenburg peasant.

"At eight o'clock the *makai* door was opened and through it came the children marching two by two and arranged according to height.

"Helene Irwan (Fagan) a most sweet little Butterfly, was the tiniest of the company and was one of the two who led the van presented to Her Majesty.

"The dances were all pretty, but the gem of the evening was number 5. It was a rare sight to see these two little ladies, Else Schaefer (Waldron) and Bessie May in their rich quaint old fashioned dresses, walk through the stately paces of the minuet. . . sober, steadfast and demure as any pensive nun could be, though merriment peeked through their eyes.

"After the minuet, supper was served in the dining room, the dancers marching in and taking assigned places, after which they were waited upon in grand style by their elders.

"The menu included the usual delicacies, and plenty of them.

"Heavy lids must have closed upon some very tired eyes last night. Never surely have any Honolulu children passed prouder hours than those which were danced away in youthful ecstacy before Hawaii's queen last night."

Four years later, this excerpt from Kate Field's description of the first auction of Palace furnishings she attended. It was June 30, 1896.

"That such a momentous event should transpire in the middle of the Pacific Ocean is due to the overthrow of the Monarchy. This sort of thing does not happen every day, or even every year, consequently Crown relics are seldom under the hammer.

" 'Why sell such things?' I ask. 'Have these men and women no heirs?'

" 'They have had more creditors than heirs,' is the reply. 'Sales of the personal effects of deceased royalty have been so common as to have been given the name of Hawaiian Opera.' "

So it seems less strange that the present government should have decided at the close of 1895 to suddenly dispose of some of the Crown china, glass, silver, and plated ware. But for the monograms and royal coat of arms, the china and glass would have no value.

"In glass cases, ranged on two sides of Morgan's mart, lay the silver, glass and china to be knocked down by the highest bidder. Silver plated dishes stood outside the case.

"First came the silver, all of which belonged to the days of Kamehameha III, most of which was marked 'KIII'.

"After the silver came a part (63 pieces) of the state china. . . white with blue border and gilt trim with the royal Hawaiian coat of arms in the center, which Dr. Judd bought for Kamehameha III when he was in Europe with the two princes.

"Mr. William G. Irwin bore it off in triumph for $252.00. The rest of the set was sold in single pieces for much more money, single plates fetching $8.00 apiece.

"After this, a similar set in white with green border, bought during Kalakaua's reign, sold equally well. Many persons were determined to possess some souvenir of a lost cause.

"The next day we gathered around the royal remains. Chipped china again brought high prices, and ordinary glass decanters sold for $18. Champagne glasses sold singly for $4 because they bore the crown and Kalakaua's monogram.

"The last aritcle sold was an ungainly solid silver centerpiece, an epergne with two matching side dishes which Kalakaua hated for obstructing the view at his dinners.

"Theo. H. Davies, the guardian of Princess Kaiulani arrived from England just in time to bid $550 and carry off the trophy that John W. Pflueger had given Kalakaua at his coronation."

Now, almost 100 years later, comes the happy ending to both these stories.

The Palace has been restored, lovingly and authentically. Its furnishings, art objects, books, the personal possessions of the rulers, jewelry, uniforms and costumes are coming home from the four corners of the globe.

Two of the Children's Ball costumes have been given, in perfect condition to the *Friends of Iolani Palace*: Lord Fauntleroys' red velvet jacket trimmed with ecru tatting with matching pants, was given by Alice Jordan Hollingsworth.

Mr. and Mrs. Charles O. Berger have given his peasant outfit. . . long cotton coat trimmed with red embroidery, large brass buttons, white shirt, knee breeches and a red silk vest.

Edward Neumann's nieces, Mrs. John Morrill and Mrs. George Sumner, have generously returned Palace silver, china, crystal and furniture.

Else Waldron returned a dance card and elaborate invitation to the ball which in those days was simply addressed Mr. and Mrs. John Doe, City.

Freddie Iaukea's descendants have been most generous, the latest item to come from them being a Hawaiian royal standard given by E.B. Watson, Jr.

Among many other things, Mrs. H. A. Walker has given two Palace arm chairs.

One of the royal beds was returned by Mr. and Mrs. James F. Morgan. . . Mr. Morgan being the grandson of the auctioneer.

The William G. Irwin Foundation sent back the original 63 pieces of blue borders of Palace china which Irwin bought at the auction, plus 33 pieces of the green and white china, a Bohemian crystal decanter with hand-engraved crown and "K", and an inlaid koa table that Helene Fagan always referred to as "the poker table my father and the King played on so often."

PALACE PARTIES

Hawaiian hospitality is world renowned, and King Kalakaua enhanced its reputation when he built Iolani Palace and entertained there on a royal scale.

The dining room seated 52, and at times as many as 75 persons. The royal tables were agleam with stately silver candelabra, silver and gold flatware, silver vegetable dishes, platters and trays. There was the elegance of Bohemian crystal, Limoges and Haviland porcelain, all engraved with the royal coat of arms or the "K" surmounted by a crown. An 1893 inventory listed 49 dozen soup spoons and 39 dozen knives.

The Royal Hawaiian band played on the verandah while the guests in full evening dress and decorations dined on mock turtle soup; boiled kumu and fried mullet; oyster pate, salmi of duck; pigeon on toast; turkey, fillet of beef and ham, shrimp and chicken curry; salad and cheese; mashed potatoes and Saratoga potatoes; green peas, and mushrooms; and finally pudding, ice cream, fruit and coffee, all washed down with the proper wines.

The Palace china, manufactured in France, dates back to the reigns of Kamehameha III, IV, and V.

During Kalakaua's reign, a firm in Boston filled orders for several dozen red, amber and blue glasses with matching finger bowls. Also, clear crystal wine glasses engraved with a crown and 110 dozen blue champagne glasses.

When the restoration of the Palace is finally completed, its air of graciousness and grandeur will be enhanced by all the original pieces that have been returned from homes in Hawaii and around the world.

Piece by piece. . . a dish here, a dish there; a glass or goblet; a fork, spoon, knife; a piece of furniture; exquisitely embroidered linens; a pair of fragile hand-blown hurricane shades, reputedly a gift of Napoleon III to Kamehameha III.

There is a bucket-shaped wine cooler with crank, wheel, and rod assembly with spring-loaded clamps to hold the cork when uncorking. "G.H. Mumm Extra Dry" is engraved on one side of it. It is said to have been a souvenir given to buyers of large orders. . . of which Kalakaua was one of the tops.

Princess Abigail Kawananakoa's grand-children have returned many familiar palace pieces that they lived with when they grew up in her home on Pensacola street.

Edward's gift of the cover for a large silver plate fish platter with the engraved "K" on one side and the crown on the other is on the shelf awaiting the return some day (hopefully) of the platter.

The silver epergne, too, will some day again grace the dining room table, with arrangements of the monarchs' favorite palapalai fern, Lokelani roses and crown flowers.

The president of the *Friends of Iolani Palace*, Kekaulike Kawananakoa, has contributed a unique silver-plated ice water cooler that may have been used in the king's chambers. The set consists of a pitcher with lid and a stand with a handle, so that when tipped the contents empty into a drinking cup on the fixed base.

Poomaikelani's elegant pair of sterling silver salt shakers and cellars engraved with the KK and crown will add the final touch of elegance to a beautifully appointed Palace banquet table.

What makes the Palace tick today? A dedicated group of volunteers working under the *Friends of Iolani Palace* and a paid staff.

The eyes and ears of the Acquisition committee members are alerted to any and all leads pertaining to former Palace possessions. Their patient and dedicated detective work has resulted in many treasures being returned, listed, authenticated, and catalogued.

Some discoveries are sheer luck, as in the case of a sharp-eyed committee member who spied a Palace chair. . . tattered and broken down. . . waiting to be picked up for the dump!

Or when a woman in Chicage read of the quest for Palace items and wrote about two green and white cake plates she had.

Queen Lilioukalani had given them to her mother and grandmother when they had called and had tea at the Plaace. She returned the two plates personally to the Palace.

If you ever feel as though a member of the *Friends of Iolani Palace* isn't 'with the conversation', look behind you. . . they may be eyeing a probable Palace piece!

COOK
A FANATIC FOR FRESH FOOD

"The Captain James Cook Bicentennial Exhibit" at the Kauai Museum is the first in the entire state. Once you have entered the museum (after nodding to the life-size model of the gentleman in the window), the set transports you back 200 years. The exhibition took 2-1/2 years of hard work and collecting with only 10 days to set up the backdrops, scenery and props.

"James Cook, ye son of a day laborer," was noted in the register of his christening in England in 1728. His childhood home made of local yellow-gray stones was shipped in 253 packing cases and reassembled in a park in Melborne, Australia in 1934.

The first signs of his life-long restlessness took him from his father's farm at the age of 17, and at 18 he went to sea as an apprentice seaman. For 33 years the sea remained his jealous mistress. In his spare time he found relaxation in the challenges the sea offered him. . . navagation, astronomy and mathematics.

He joined the Royal Navy at 27, and married Elizabeth Batts seven years later. We found nothing of their courtship. . . lengthy or spontaneous. . . and Elizabeth remains a shadowy figure waiting for a fiction writer with wild imagination. She is noted to have said, however, she preferred Nathaniel Dance's portrait of Cook over Webber's, but why?

Cook wrote reams in great detail. . . ships' logs and letters but barely mentioned his wife or even a hint of losing his children. Elizabeth Batts Cook is an enigma. . . an inscrutable part of Cook's unwritten life.

The newlyweds bought a home on Mile End Road and chose furniture for it from the shops of the artisans of the day. . . Messieurs Thomas Chippendale, Thomas Sheraton and George Hepplewhite.

Four months after their marriage Cook returned to his first love, the sea, and embarked on the Newfoundland Survey which was used as standard guide for all seamen for the following 100 years. As skipper of his first ship, even though still not a commissioned officer, he began his persistent fight against the deadly maritime disease, scurvy.

A picture of the Copley Gold Medal awarded Cook by the Royal Society in 1776 is evidence of his election to membership in this exclusive group of intellectual and scientific men. His winning paper on the prevention of scurvy stressed the importance of fresh food, the value of malts and conserves, fresh water, and personal hygiene with clothes and quarters clean and dry at all times. His insistence on lots of rest led to a revised watch of 4 hours duty and 8 hours off so that men could have uninterrupted sleep at sea as on land.

Captian Cook knew whereof he wrote. Through the years of his voyages of discovery Cook was a stickler for fresh food. . . even grass if necessary. . . and water. Fresh food and water had top priority when he beached his small boats.

Taking on native fresh produce served two purposes. . . the prevention of scurvy, and saving the supply of salt meat, oatmeal and ship's buscuits. His providing of these fresh supplies resulted in a healthy crew with high morale. . . a rarity in the Navy.

Water was a precious commodity. Strict naval rules limited the washing of hands and face and laundry but Cook put no rationing on drinking water for his men.

A good example of this is found in the Endeavor's journey in 1768 when the ship reached Madeira. The crew had visions of cask after cask of golden wines, but Cook's sole purpose in landing was fresh food and water!

He made straight for the native markets and loaded the little ship with fresh beef and chickens, bananas, mangoes, guavas, and 3,000 pounds of onions! Each man was consigned 20 pounds of onions, like it or not, and Cook led the mass-crying jag to good health.

Because of her captain's disbelief in Cook's fanticism for fresh foods, the accompanying ship *Adventurer* was struck with cases of scurvy. Cook sent over a new cook with strict orders to feed the men fresh wort (malt unfermented or in fermentation), preserve of carrots and essence of lemon until they gagged, but lived!

Cook remained a non-commissioned officer until August 1768. In those days officers and gentlemen were born, not made, and that left out Cook, the son of a laborer. He lived very much unto himself. . . in his own private world. . . and yet he was a great leader, courageous, and ever daring to venture in uncharted waters. He well earned the sobriquet, King of Navigators.

The Royal Navy commissioned him a lieutenant and picked him to lead the first voyage to seek new lands. Food for a complement of nearly a hundred men had to last at least two years. A healthy supply of salt pork and biscuits and preserved sauerkraut was basic. He insisted on the sauerkraut to fight scurvy and a goat to supply fresh milk. Men were flogged for not adhering to his strict diet routine!

A photo of a painting by Sir Joshua Reynolds of a Tahitian lad, Omai, has an interesting background. The captain of the *Adventurer* brought this young lad back from Tahiti on the second voyage and he became the spoiled darling of English and French societies, was presented at Court, and became a great favorite of the ladies!

In 1776 this same Omai was the published reason for the third journey from England. He was to be returned to Tahiti. Cook sailed on board the *Resolution* with 22-year old William Bligh as sailing master. A draftsman, James Webber, was assigned the task of 'ship's photographer', to sketch the new sights and people they encountered. Several of his oils on loan hang in the museum exhibit.

The *Resolution* was Cook's real home as he spent more time aboard her than at Mile End Road. The comparison of the *Resolution*, 110 feet 8 inches long and 401 tons to the present *Mariposa,* 563 feet long and 20,600 tons gives you a good idea of the available space on board! His aft cabin had seven windows overlooking the wake and was furnished with a round table and straight back chairs.

Years on his father's farm taught him how to keep the menagerie of cattle, pigs, sheep, and goats alive through all kinds of weather, and he even took on four horses at Capetown. This livestock along with various seeds were to be presented to the natives of various islands on behalf of the agricultural-minded King George.

Serving with Captain Charles Clerke on board the accompanying brig, *Discovery,* was an 18 year-old midshipman, George Vancouver.

On January 18, 1778, Cook sighted the islands of Oahu, Kauai, and Niihau and sailed into Waimea Bay on Kauai. The natives came out to visit this strange apparition and trading began with small nails or pieces of iron for fish and sweet potato.

Captain Cook quickly made for shore in search of much-needed water and was met by a dignified leader surrounded by natives waving branches of sugar cane like umbrellas. Much to his delight Cook found Kauai to be a most cooperative and hospitable island with an abundance of fresh meat and vegetables.

He grew to love the Hawaiians best of all the natives he had known in this travels. He trusted them. They were generous and kind. He had been away from England 3-1/2 years and barter goods were running low but yet these people gave unstintingly of their food and animals.

His death at Kealakekua Bay is history, but it is amazing to note that he was unable to reach the longboat because this great sailor, this discoverer of so many new worlds, had never learned to swim.

In place of Cook's original sauerkraut recipe, I prevailed upon the director of this extravaganza to give us his very own cabbage recipe: Bob Gahram's Ginger Slaw, see page 21.

SALT PONDS OF HANAPEPE

A trip to Hanapepe salt ponds is a humbling experience. There you will see a *hui* of hard-working, dedicated people. . . each in his own *kuleana*. . . preserving a facet of Hawaiian culture.

Making salt still involves the back-breaking work it did over a hundred years ago when the king granted this land for Hawaiians in Hanapepe to work as salt ponds.

In the old days the *akua-aina* (priestess) prayed for guidance and when the time was right, called the people to open the season with prayers and a *paina* (a meal usually consisting of a small pig). The salt workers still gather to pray and share food to open the season. No smoking or drinking of alcohol is allowed on the premises.

Helen Chu, whose husband's grandmother was an original owner of one of the *kuleanas*, kindly guided me through the working of the ponds. The season opens in May about the time the marshy waters recede and runs through September when the hot summer sun is best for harvesting. Rains dilute the salt water forming the crystals, and delay the harvesting.

Today it is amazing to behold such anti-quated operations. With a crude piece of iron the workers re-form the beds, removing all excess mud by hand to form a retaining wall and using the wet clay as plaster. The 6 ft. by 4 ft. beds must be absolutely leakproof and level and the final smoothing process is done with a large smooth stone dipped in and out of water.

The beds are left to dry under a hot sun for 1 to 2 hours. As a potter perfects his coffee cup without any bubbles before firing, so the beds must be crack-proof. Imagine perfecting a dozen beds!

Each *kuleana* has its own *puna wai*, a deep well. It is the source of brackish water which is brought up by rope attached to old buckets or tin cans tied to bamboo poles to fill the *waiku*, a curing pond where water stands for 3 to 4 days before it is transferred to the *aina*, the drying basin.

The *aina* is filled with about 3 or 4 inches to start, and after 3 days, crystals which resemble snow flakes and sparkling diamonds begin to form and float to the surface. These beds. . . five, eight, ten or twelve of them. . . must be checked every day, and if the sun is really hot and evaporation takes place faster, the workers must add two inches more water from the *waiku* every other day.

When three inches of pure salt forms it is time to harvest. The salt is pushed by long-handled home-made rakes to the ends of the beds and gathered up in bamboo baskets. If the crystals are dirty, the salt is washed in the *waiku* thereby strengthening that supply.

By tossing the salt in the basket and rubbing the large crystals together in the palms of the hands, the workers break it down into smaller bits. Piled in a big mound, it is left to dry for a week and then bagged.

And after all this hard work the salt is not sold! However, there is a big demand for the Hanapepe salt, and a bargaining set up works out beautifully. You have pigs, chickens, fish, rice, taro, vegetables, guava jelly and want salt. . . the salt-maker needs what you have. . . so you simply barter and trade and everyone is oh so happy! Yep, today in little downtown Hanapepe!

Pa-a-kai, Hawaiian rock salt, has always been one of the main staples of the Hawaiians not only for food but for medicinal purposes, too. Hawaiian salt mixed in a tumbler of warm water is still used to gargle for a sore throat.

I can remember my grandmother giving a man a glass of the salt mixed in warm water after a fall from the roof.

Pain from a smashed finger was relieved by soaking in hot, hot water with lots of salt several times a day. And for those who haven't been horseback riding for quite a while, a glass of warm water with a teaspoon of salt taken when you get home and. . . no *eha ovah heah!* (Not stiff, *na hoi!*)

Even animals were treated. . . if a cow or pig had a sprained leg and couldn't walk, a solution of warm water mixed with salt was used to wash the leg every morning and evening. Pure salt was rubbed on the cut and not only healed but kept the flies off.

In many Island homes a container of *Pa-a-kai* on the table is preferred for its taste and flavor. Many Island cooks use the *pa-a-kai* exclusively in cooking and are firmly convinced it is far superior to the 'haole salt'.

Whole fish sprinkled generously with salt and put to dry in a hot sun for a day or two keeps for weeks in a covered jar. Always rub pineapple with *Pa-a-kai* before slicing, and kids love peeled half-ripe mangoes with Hawaiian salt. . . cuts the acid.

PAPAYAS

Two vivid childhood memories come back at the mention of papaya. We used to string lovely leis from the creamy white fragrant blossoms. . . but only from the male tree.

The female tree provided the luscious orange fruit that constituted every *kamaaina's* breakfast. (Today, of course. . . and such is progress. . . the solo variety of papaya produces a hermaphrodite tree which fertilizes itself and bears fruit without requiring a grove of neighbors.)

Papaya and Kona coffee for breakfast was an Island institution in every household. In the more elegant homes, dowagers speared the end of their papaya with a fork and scooped out the flesh with a very shiny silver spoon. This was followed by a finger bowl to rinse off any sticky traces.

In the old days housewives (or their cooks) tenderized fresh meat by wrapping it in green papaya leaves and leaving it to stand overnight. The old-timers instinctively knew the fruit's valuable digestive properties and that it was full of vitamin A and C especially.

Today we know that the milky juice contains papain which resembles pepsin and is used in various medical preparations. So it behooves us to nuture papaya trees in our own back yards.

PAPAYA SEED DRESSING

Papaya Seed Dressing is good but sweet and you don't really taste the seeds. . . more like an Italian dressing.

In a blender container place 3/4 C salad oil, 1/3 C tarragon vinegar, 1 T lime juice, 1/4 C sugar, 2 t minced onions, 1/2 t each salt, dry mustard, and 1/4 t paprika.

Cover and blend at high speed 1 to 2 minutes, add 1-1/2 T papaya seeds and blend till seeds resemble coarsely ground pepper and mixture thickens. Cover and chill. Shake well before serving over fruit or tossed vegetable salads.

This Papaya Seed Dressing uses mayonnaise and you can add it to any salad mix served in papaya halves.

Blend 1/2 C mayonnaise, 1 T papaya seeds, 1 t lime juice, 1/16 t each ground ginger and cayenne until seeds are consistency of coarse pepper. Add 1/3 C chopped tomato and serve as dressing with salad.

PAPAYA ICE CREAM SAUCE

Blend 1 C Grand Marnier and 1/4 C brown sugar. Pour over 1-1/2 quarts sliced papaya in shallow dish and chill. Keep turning fruit in liquid during marinating. Sprinkle with macadamia nut brittle and serve over ice cream.

MACADAMIA NUT BRITTLE

Chop nuts fine. In large skillet heat 2 C sugar slowly, stirring occasionally until sugar melts and turns a light golden brown. Quickly stir in nuts and turn into an oiled pan and let stand until cold. Crush brittle into fine crumbs.

PAPAYA FRITTERS

Beat 2 eggs, 2 T milk and 1/2 t salt together just until blended. . . don't overbeat. Peel, halve and de-seed 2 papayas and cut into large chunks and pat dry.

Dip into egg mixture then roll in crumbs mixed with sesame seeds. Deep fry in hot oil 3 to 5 minutes until golden brown.

Serve with *Lemon Cream Sauce*.

Blend 1 T grated lemon rind and 2 T sugar into 2 C whipped cream and garnish with cinnamon.

PAPAYA SLUSH

Papaya Slush is great on a hot day. Combine in blender container 1 papaya, peeled and de-seeded, 1 orange, peeled and quartered, 1 C plain yogurt, 1/4 C brown sugar, juice of 1 lemon, and 1/2 t cinnamon. Blend on high speed until smooth. Stir in 1 C ginger ale, pour into glasses and garnish with mint or strawberry.

PAPAYA CUSTARD

Mix 4 C ripe papaya pulp with 1 C shredded coconut and spread in bottom of buttered 2 quart souffle dish.

Scald 1 quart light cream with a piece of vanilla bean, then discard bean. Beat 6 eggs with 1/4 t salt and 1/4 C sugar and pour into the hot cream, stirring well. When sugar is dissolved, stir in juice, grated rind and pulp of 1 medium size orange.

Pour mixture over papaya and coconut, place dish in a pan of warm water and bake in 350 oven about 35 minutes until blade of knife comes out clean. Custard thickens when it cools. Serve with guava jelly and thin papaya slices.

PAPAYA RELISH

This Relish can be used as a condiment for broiled meats or curry or as a salad over lettuce.

Peel 1 large, ripe, firm papaya, remove seeds, shred coarsely on grater. Combine with 1/2 t grated green ginger, 1 t salt, 2 T lemon juice, and 1 canned peeled green chili, chopped.

ALL YOU WANT TO KNOW ABOUT TARO AND POI

Taro is considered a rather fattening commodity, probably because of the portly Hawaiian race. However, in David Malo's book, *Hawaiian Antiquities*, he says that the origin of *taro* goes back to a frail child.

In the creation legend of Papa and Wakea, their first child was a prematurely born son whom they named Haloa-Naka. He did not survive, and they buried him at one end of their house.

There in the same spot a *taro* plant shot up, and they called the stem of the strange plant Haloa. This was the name they gave their second son who, legend tells, was the progenitor of all the peoples of the earth.

From these bits of legend and myth we can better understand the meaning of *taro* as the Hawaiian staff of life. . . root, stem, and leaf.

In the Monarchy period, the *taro* leaf was important as a design motif and it was used only by royalty, forbidden to the commoner.

Kamehameha III's vest was heavily embroidered with wire of gold bullion in the *taro* leaf design. Later, the collars and cuffs of the court uniforms were embellished in the same pattern.

A finely engraved scroll of *taro* leaves runs along the gilt sheath of Kalakaua's court sword. The same engraving is found on his belt and the coronation crown.

Panels in the glass doors of Iolani Palace were decorated with the engraved *taro* leaf design and one of the Palace sofas features a taro leaf design on the frame.

Today, *taro* is becoming scarce and *poi* (made from *taro*) is not always available.

The staff of life to Hawaiians, *poi* is a nutritious addition to babies' diets, enjoyed by *kamaainas*, gingerly dipped into once, at least, by *malihinis*, sometimes referred to as paper hanger's glue, but it's still the piece de resistance at a *luau*.

Taro contains a high concentration of calcium oxalate in the form of needle-like crystals that can cause severe itching if the corms and leaves are not properly prepared and cooked.

Taro corms can be boiled in the skin after a scrubbing, or they can be peeled, but the water should be changed several times. Boil in water to cover, and test for doneness like potato.

After the *taro* is thoroughly cooked, you have many options. Cut the peeled *taro* in 1/2 inch slices, sprinkle with salt (flour is optional) and fry quickly in butter until crispy and brown.

TARO CHIPS

For Taro Chips, slice the peeled cooked *taro* as thin as possible and deep fry it in hot oil until crisp. Drain on brown paper and sprinkle with salt.

TARO CAKES

For Taro Cakes, boil the peeled *taro* until very tender, almost mushy. Mash until smooth while still hot, using as little water as possible. To one C mashed *taro* add 1 t each baking powder and salt and 1 T sugar. Wet your hands and form the mixture into small cakes.

Place them on buttered cookie sheet, press in a pat of butter on top of each and bake in 350 oven for about 20 minutes or until brown.

Or you may put the mixture into small buttered muffin tins and bake 10 to 15 minutes until they are puffy and brown.

For a delicious *pupu*, make taro cakes as usual, but only add salt. Mix in broken up bits of cooked Portuguese sausage and chopped green onions. Form into small balls and bake in hot oven until crispy and brown. Serve hot.

Used cooked *taro* in stew instead of potatoes. It tends to thicken the stew, too. Or use *poi* to thicken your stew instead of flour and water.

Slather *poi* over a bee bite. It relieves the sting and throbbing.

Unfortunately, the *poi* available today is not the thick glutinous mass it used to be and for some reason it takes longer to sour. . . if at all.

To mix *poi*. Open bag, fill it with water and, holding it securely closed, loosen the *poi* from the sides of the bag. Carefully drain out all the water and then slip the contents into a large, wet bowl.

The only way to properly mix *poi* is by hand, adding a little water at a time until it reaches the right consistency. . . which isn't too watery.

After mixing, be sure and *kahi* (wipe down the sides of the bowl) *poi*, and sprinkle the top with water to keep it from drying out and forming a crust.

The leaves of the *taro* plant must be cleaned and prepared carefully, too.

Snip off an inch at each end of the *luau* leaf, peel the fiber off the main large stem and down the veins, and then wash thoroughly.

Stuff the leaves into a large pot, add lots of water and let it boil. It soon cooks down to almost nothing.

Let it boil for an hour, then drain, rinse, cover with fresh water, and boil until easily cut with spoon or fork. Rinse and drain well.

See page 41 for recipe for delicious Chicken Luau.

GOING BANANAS OVER BANANAS

The early migrators to Hawaii brought the roots and shoots of one of the most prolific tropical plants with them. . . the banana or *mai'a*. Before the tabus were broken in 1819, women were not allowed to eat certain types of bananas.

Even today Hawaiian superstition still persists. It's bad luck for fishermen to have bananas with them, or even dream of bananas! It is referred to as the "tree of birth and life" or "Life out of death", for as the fruit destroys the plant so new plants spring up from the old stumps.

Once planted, the banana plant is difficult to get rid of and needs protection from strong winds during its nine-month growing cycle. The fruit is rich in carbohydrates and proteins. In choosing bananas, look for hands of yellow fruit with green tips.

To hasten the ripening process, place them in a brown bag and leave in dark spot. They are best eaten when the fruit is solid yellow with brown flecks. Cooking bananas should never be eaten raw.

There are several different varieties of delicious eating bananas. . . Chinese (a dwarf type), Bluefield, apple, red, ice cream, and lady fingers.

For serving remove the fibrous strings and dip in lemon juice to keep from turning dark. Actually, it enhances the flavor, too.

Try combining mashed bananas with peanut butter for a nummy sandwich.

Slice them thin into your favorite pancake or waffle recipe.

Bake cooking bananas whole and serve in the skins, but remove both ends. Cook 20 minutes in 350 oven and slit open to douse with butter.

If you have an overabundance of ripe bananas, pop them into a zip lock bag and freeze them until you're ready to fry or mash for batter.

BANANA CHIPS

For Banana Chips peel not quite ripe bananas, slice very thick, spread on a towel and dust lightly with flour. Fry in deep fat like potato chips until a delicate brown. Drain on brown paper and sprinkle with salt.

CHOCOLATE COVERED BANANAS

Kiddies and adults, too, love Chocolate Covered Bananas. Insert lollipop sticks lengthwise into firm banana. Melt semi-sweet chocolate bars and when cool, dip the banana into mixture to coat completely. Set on wax paper to harden and keep in freezer.

BROILED BANANAS

Wrap pieces of firm bananas with bacon or ham strips and hold together securely with toothpicks. Broil at 375 for 4 minutes on each side or until pork is done and crispy.

BANANA FRENCH TOAST

Beat 2 eggs with 1/2 C sugar and then add 1 small can coconut milk. Stir in 2 well mashed bananas, 1 t vanilla, 1/4 t salt and mix well until smooth.

Heat frying pan and pour in ample oil when hot. Dip slices of bread on both sides in batter and fry until golden brown and done on each side. Drain on brown paper and serve hot.

BANANA OATMEAL MUFFINS

Mix 1 C quick cooking oatmeal, 1 small mashed banana and 1/2 C sour milk together. Add 1 beaten egg and 1/4 C brown sugar.

Sift 1 C flour, 1 t each baking powder and salt, 1/2 t baking soda and add to mixture. Cool 1/3 C melted shortening and stir into batter. Fill greased muffin tins 2/3 full and bake at 400 degrees for 15-20 minutes.

BANANA BREAD PUDDING

Soak 2 C stale bread crumbs (no crusts) in 2 C scalded milk and cool. Add 1 mashed banana, 2 T sugar, 1/4 C melted butter, 1/2 t salt and 2 eggs slightly beaten. Pour in greased pudding dish, place in pan of hot water, and bake 1 hour at 325 degrees.

BANANA CREAM PIE

In top of double boiler beat 3 eggs slightly with 1/4 C sugar and a pinch of salt. Add 2 C scalded milk gradually and keep stirring until mixture coats spoon. Add 1/2 t vanilla. Cool.

Bake a pie shell and fill it with 2 C sliced bananas (1/2 inch thick). Pour the cooled custard over the bananas, chill in refrigerator and serve with whipped cream.

RUM BANANAS

Peel 8 bananas and cut in half lengthwise, place flat side down in pan and dribble 4 T melted oleo, 1/2 C brown sugar and 1/2 C either lime or orange juice over them. Add enough rum to coat bananas completely. Bake in 250 degree oven for 20 minutes and keep basting. Put under broiler for about 2-3 minutes to brown slightly. Serve with ice cream or whipped cream.

A TURN OF THE CENTURY LOOK AT THE HAWAIIAN FISH MARKET

Browsing thru some musty ole papers the other day, I came across the following from the 1898 issue of "Paradise of the Pacific".

"The Honolulu fish market on Saturday afternoon is the time and place to see Hawaiian belledom. It is the day above all others when femininity, decked in its little best, preens itself on parade and celebrates the end of the week. There is no better place than the fish market in which to study the peculiar gait of the Hawaiian women. No other women in the world swing massive frames on slender feet in quite the way that these women do. There is a peculiar motion of the shoulder, a graceful movement to the hip, which combined with fine, strong straight backs. . . legacies from centuries when there were no chairs in Hawaii... give these women the most graceful and distinguished carriage in the world.

"The stalls themselves have passed almost entirely into the hands of the Chinese, who have a smattering of Hawaiian and stretch out their hands full of struggling, fluttering, flopping fish! A steady stream of natives clutch their purchases. . . each fish bound about the middle with a *ti* leaf, its head and tail protruding. Wrapping paper is almost unknown in the fish market. Everything is picturesquely swathed in the green and glossy *ti* leaves. At a *luau* everything that is not cooked in *ti* leaves is served on them. The Hawaiians would not know how to keep house without them!

"Mullet is the great standby of Honolulu... the most plentiful and the cheapest and also one of the best. The Hawaiians prize several varieties of seaweed. It is a cultivated taste like that for caviar, and they both have the same briny taste of the ocean."

FISH PUDDING

That was back in 1898. One of the favorite ladies' luncheon dishes back then was *Fish Pudding*, which we can make today with prepared raw fish cake. Scrape 3 pounds raw fish, season with salt and pepper and add 4 egg yolks one at a time. When all mixed, add 1/2 C bread crumbs and 3/4 C cream, then the stiffly beaten 4 egg whites. Place in well-buttered steaming mold, cover tightly and place in boiling water to simmer for 1/2 hour. Serve with rich cream sauce.

FISHY TIPS

If you do have fresh fish here are a few fishy tips. Test fish like a cake. . . use a toothpick to test for doneness. Do not overcook or it will lose its delicate flavor.

If you squeeze lemon juice on both sides of the fish and let it marinate for an hour before cooking, it will improve the flavor and help keep the fish smell from permeating the house.

Be sure your skillet or grill is hot and well greased when you put in the fish, otherwise it will stick and break.

If fresh fish isn't available for one reason or another scan these canned options.

CRABMEAT BURGERS

Mix well: 1 7-1/2 ounce can crab, 1/2 pound grated cheddar cheese, 1 small onion grated, 2 T mayonnaise and 1 can tomato soup. Spread on slightly toasted hamburger buns and bake at 350 or broil until light brown and bubbly.

WIKIWIKI MAHI CHOWDER

Cook 1 pound skinned mahimahi in water to cover for 10 minutes. Remove meat and de-bone if necessary. Cook 2 large potatoes cut in 1 inch cubes and 1 large onion chopped fine in fish water and when cooked add 1 can cream of mushroom soup and dilute with milk if too thick. Add flaked fish and heat over low heat for five minutes.

FANCY CRAB SANDWICH

Drain 1 7-1/2 ounce can crab and cut or shred. Cream 1 3-ounce softened package cream cheese with 2 T mayonnaise and 2-3 T minced green onion, 1/4 C thinly sliced celery, 1 t lemon juice, dash of Worcestershire sauce, seasoning to taste and the crab. Mix well and make sandwiches with 12 slices of day-old bread.

Beat together 2 eggs, 2/3 C milk and dash of salt and pepper. Put in shallow dish and dip both sides of each sandwich in this and bake on lightly greased grill or skillet until golden brown. Serve hot.

CRAB OR TUNA SOUFFLE

Dice 4 slices bread into greased casserole and moisten with milk. Mix together: 1/4 C mayonnaise, 2 beaten eggs, 1/2 can mushroom soup, 2 cans crab or tuna, 1/2 C chopped onion, 1 C each chopped parsley and green pepper, 1 C grated cheddar cheese, 2 t paprika, 1/2 t dill weed, t lemon juice and add to casserole. Sprinkle with bread crumbs, bake 45 minutes to an hour in 350 oven or until knife comes out clean.

TUNA CREOLE IN RICE RING

In 2 T oil saute 1/2 C each chopped green pepper, onion and celery, 1 clove crushed garlic until tender. Add 1 2-ounce can tomato paste, 1-1/4 C water, 1 bay leaf, 1 t each salt and dill weed, dash of tabasco and simmer 30 minutes. Stir occasionally. Add 2 6-1/2 to 7-1/2 ounce cans chunk style tuna, drained and flaked, to heat through. Pack 4 C hot cooked rice in buttered ring mold and turn onto serving platter. Fill the center with the Tuna Creole. Makes 4 servings.

TUNA SOUFFLE SANDWICH

Blend 1 can grated tuna, 1/2 t dill weed, 1 T each minced onion and lemon juice and spread evenly on untoasted side of 6 slices of bread. Mix 1/4 C mayonnaise with 1 stiffly beaten egg white and cover the fish mixture. Place under the broiler until it is a delicate brown.

ORANGE-TOMATO CRAB

In skillet cook 1 chopped onion and 1 green pepper sliced, in 2 T oil until tender. Stir in 1 6-ounce can tomato paste, 3/4 C orange juice, 1/2 C water, 2 T sliced pimientos, 1 T brown sugar (packed), and 1 t salt. Simmer 10 minutes. Stir in 12 ounces cooked canned or frozen crab and simmer only until crab is heated through. Garnish with orange sections and serve with hot rice or hot buttered sour dough bread.

AUNTIE POEPE SAYS "ALOHA NO-O-O-O, HALEKULANI"

Dear Maili:

"Howayu? Long time no see!

The otha day, I was sweeping undah the hikie'e, weeshing we could go holo holo some place foah dinnah.

"Eh, Papa."

"Uuugh,"

I thought he only reading the papah on top the couch, I nevah no he hiamoe.

"Let's go Halekulani Hotel."

"Whut you saying?"

"I say, let's go Halekulani Hotel. Whea you romance? How can you fowget all those happy days? Pretty soon all pau."

He went look long time at the flooah, then his face light up with one big smile.

"Aloha no, Halekulani! Mama, if not foa my ole boss, that hansum Waltah Dillingham, auwee, no moah Halekulani Hotel, I tell you."

"Howcum?"

"Waltah went fah away to school Newton, Massachewsets and he made good frens with one young fella living ovah thea. When time foah come home, he said, 'Clifford, if you evah like come Hawaii, you come stay with me. I show you the islands.'

"Wot you know! Couple eas latah Clifford Kimball went visit Waltah. Then he see Juliet King, one of the belles of Honolulu, and they marry.

"By'n bye these two, and then thea sons, Keoki and Kingie went make the Halekulani Hotel.

"Okay, Mama we go! We go say goodbye Halekulani."

We got all dolled up, stop Maunakea street so he can buy me one gingah lei, and off we go.

Nowadays have to go slow by easy through all that traffic, I tell you. Not like the old days. . . along King street, out Kalakaua, down Lewers and right into the hotel grouns and pahk undah the coconut trees.

But some nice boy pahk the kaa for us, and I look aroun at all the cottages. . . jes like one manini village inside one concrete jungle!

Then I think I see Aunt Juliet Kimball sitting thea on her lanai with the red caladiums in full bloom on the steps. How many times we used to sit with her talking plans for the Dottahs of Hawaii when she regent or sewing guild at the cathedral! Plenty talk-talk but time for nana the tourists walking by, too.

We walk aroun, look all the hibiscus plants Aunt Juliet planted and loved. The grouns like one living memorial for her.

We went roun the main building and the little Japanee fish pond, and Papa head right for the House Without a Key.

I so busy looking all the sailboats, catamarans, surfahs, and canoes, I almos bang my haid on the hau tree limb.

We sat down undah the famous kiawe tree and queek the pretty waitress cum ask what we like drink. You bet you life I say, 'Mai Tai, please' jes like that. . . like ole times! Papa orday his beeah and then we look aroun, evrybudy so relaxed.

Pretty soon I notice Papa not looking me, so I follow his makas to the stone wall. . . some parade!

Those wahines passing by shua get the figahs. Jes like my hi-school moopuna. . . foah jus that leetle bit cloth they pay big money an no like eat nothing! Those suits not made foah paddling a canoe or surfing koa boards like how we used to do. . . now only foah look.

Then the girls went sing, "Haleiwa", an you see Papa like sing along.

"Auwe, aloha no Haleiwa. . . the Kimball's first hotel, Papa says.

"I remembah when I running the Dillingham's trains and we stop Haleiwa, let off the hotel guests. I toot the whistle and those little Kimball keikis cum running outside to wave!

"One day Aunt Juliet saw one small ad in the papah. . . 'a going hotel with 3 cottages an main building with 8-9 rooms and a beautiful hau tree.'

"Cum to fine out it was the Robert Lewer's old beach house. I can remembah Granpa telling us how they used to beach thea canoes up ovah theah. . . the ewa side by the honeymoon cottage. Ai, it was those ole Hawaiians who gave the name Halekulani, by golly."

You know Papa. . . he so sentimental. But so interesting how he remembah all how Mr. Clifford Kimball finally leased the hotel aroun 1917. When the lease pau in 1928, the Kimballs save like anything to buy the property and that's when they build the main building.

Must have been roun the '30's. . . ho, was jus like one beautiful home with all the koa furnicher, paintings by all the ole timers like Howard Hitchcock. . . an you see all those kamaaina matriachs living there so happy! Mrs. Batten, Clifford's sister, Helen Kimball,

Mrs. Renjes, the Ray Colls, Mrs. Hedemann. . . so happy.

Whea the cottages are now, ah, that was a house whea Jack London and his lovalee wife, Charmaigne lived. He so hansum and smaht foa write stories, too.

Then Mrs. Edward Groenendyke leased the house, too, and fun look the pitchas her son Eddie's widow has of those old days. . . you see Kingie, Keoki, Lowell Dillingham, and Eddie Groenendyke showing off on the lawn undah the kiawe tree, and only Diamon Head in the background.

I went look inside the main dining room and remembah the first black-out dances during the wah. That's when the bahbed wia all strung out along the sea wall.

In wah or peace, the Kimball family always like see everybudy happy. An for shua those Navy fellas relax, I tell you.

Got so wela inside Kingie and his wife, Mary, went change the dances outside in the House Without a Key. Oh, so romantic. . . only the moonlight dancing on the watah and no can light even one cigeret.

We had flaming Cherries Jubilee an champagne to toast the Kimballs and that Norton Clapp man from Tacoma for keeping their aloha and hospitality alive as long as he could.

You wait. . . when the new hotel all pau, we all go and have good times one moah time.

The blue and green watah still dance when the moon cum up ovah Diamon Head. You can still reach up and pick a stah to weave your lei.

The sun will always set in a blaze of glorious colors ovah the Waianae mountains, and hopefully the sassy sparrows will return to nestle in the hau trees and snap your popovahs when you not looking!

Aloha no-o-o-o-o-o Halekulani!

Auntie Poepe

THE ABC's OF A HAWAIIAN GARDEN

Do you remember playing that old game, "In my grandmother's trunk there was a. . .?" We used to play it with the children to keep a little peace on long rides home from the country.

Somehow it came back as a challenge to see if I could fill not only the old trunk but a Hawaiian garden. Fill it with plants for beauty, smell, nutrition and nostalgia and so here we go! Maybe you can fill another garden with your own Hawaiian Plants.

Aloe for treating burns and avocados for their butter-like quality.

Bananas. . . raw, baked, fried, baked in breads and cakes and don't ever forget all that potassium.

Citrus, all kinds of oranges, limes and lemons, pomelos and grapefruit, too.

Day lilies, a long border up a winding driveway of the orange, lemon-yellow and brown and orange varieties to remind me of the old homes in the valleys.

Elepaio bird to enjoy as it darts through my garden.

Fig tree to wrap in netting when the luscious fruit appear and ripen on the branch.

Guava tree for juice and preserves and grapes to cover an arbor as in days of yore and maybe to brew wine today!

Hala trees, lovely to behold and the source

of an almost forgotten Hawaiian craft.

Ixora bushes, lots of the old-fashioned red variety to fill the house with massive bouquets, and ilima bushes to remind me of the alii.

Java plum trees, messy as they are, can make a staunch wind-break, and you get delightful jelly from the fruit.

Kukui trees for their distinctive green color and the nuts so chock full of protein and uses.

Lilikoi vines for lots of juice and pies and laukahi, my favorite Hawaiian herb with so many uses.

Mango trees towering and laden with fruit for chutney and pies, mulberry tree for old time's sake and mountain apple tree for the brillant feathery blossoms and watery fruit.

Noni for the medicinal properties the Hawaiians treasured.

Ohia tree with its wispy red lehua blossoms to tempt the fates and pick in defiance of the rains.

Puakinikini tree for leis of its waxy ivory flowers that turn orange, palapali fern for more leis and papaya for our daily fruit.

Quince, the flowering variety to cut and bring in the house to herald spring.

Rose apple tree for its delicate-flavored friut.

Soursop tree for luscious sherbets and sugar cane, just a small clump like all the old homes used to have.

Taro and ti, the mainstays of the Hawaiians.

Ulu, the breadfruit tree and its fruit, which needs an acquired taste.

Violets, borders of purple and white blossoms hidden among the rich green leaves waiting to be picked.

Wi tree with its prickly-centered fruit you seldom see today.

X to mark the spot for contemplation in the garden.

Yesterday-today-tomorrow bush with its white, lavender and purple flowers ever changing.

Zinnias, beds of multi-colored flowers like the old mama-sans used to wrap in newspaper, stuff their baskets and vend for a quarter chanting "Farawah, farawah!"

Oh what a happy retreat of memories and beauty this garden would be!!

....Index....

. . . . Notes . . . .